HE CALLED
HER

HE CALLED HER

PENTECOSTAL WOMEN IN MINISTRY

DANIEL J. KOREN

WAP Academic

WAP ACADEMIC
A Division of Word Aflame Press
8855 Dunn Road, Hazelwood, MO 63042
www.pentecostalpublishing.com

© 2016 by Daniel J. Koren

All rights reserved. No portion of this publication may be reproduced, stored in an electronic system, or transmitted in any form or by any means, electronic, mechanical, photocopy, recording, or otherwise, without the prior permission of Word Aflame Press. Brief quotations may be used in literary reviews.

All Scripture verses quoted are from the New King James Version unless otherwise identified.

New King James Version © 1982 by Thomas Nelson, Inc. Used by permission. All rights reserved.

Scripture verses marked (ESV) from the ESV Bible (The Holy Bible, English Standard Version), © 2001 by Crossway, a publishing ministry of Good News Publishers. Used by permission. All rights reserved.

Printed in the United States of America.

Cover Design: Elizabeth Loyd

Library of Congress Cataloging-in-Publication Data

Names: Koren, Daniel, 1977- author.
Title: He called her : Pentecostal women in ministry / Daniel J. Koren.
Description: Hazelwood : Word Aflame Press, 2016. | Includes bibliographical references.
Identifiers: LCCN 2016017324 | ISBN 9780757749308 (alk. paper)
Subjects: LCSH: Women clergy. | Pentecostal churches--Doctrines. | Women in church work--Pentecostal churches. | Sex role--Religious aspects--Pentecostal churches.
Classification: LCC BV676 .K67 2016 | DDC 261/.14994082--dc23 LC record available at https://lccn.loc.gov/2016017324

To Judith "AJ" Walker

who was not afraid

to be a pioneer

Contents

Foreword – Janice Sjostrand............................ ix

Preface xi

Acknowledgements.......................................xiii

He Called Junia: Women as Missionaries 1
Is the idea of women in ministry a new thing?

He Called Mary: Women as Evangelists 17
Can a woman preach the gospel?

He Called Anna: Women as Prophets 29
Does I Corinthians 14:34–35 silence women in church?

He Called Deborah: Women as Leaders 47
Can women serve only when a man does not respond to the call?

He Called Priscilla: Women as Teachers 59
Can a woman teach Bible truths?

He Called Sarah: Women as Daughters 73
Does I Timothy 2:11–12 prohibit women from teaching men?

He Called Esther: Women in Authority 89
Can a woman have authority in the church?

He Called Phoebe: Women as Ministers 103
Can a woman be a licensed/ordained minister?

He Called Lydia: Women as Pastors 115
Can a woman be a pastor?

He Called Eve: Women as Ladies 131
Must women be submitted to men to do ministry?

He Called Ruth: Women as Wives 147
Is a wife subjected to her husband?

He Called Tabitha: Women as Role-models 169
Where does a woman get started in ministry?

Notes 179

Bibliography 199

Scripture Index 205

Foreword
by Janice Sjostrand

I met Daniel Koren through his six-year-old daughter Esther, whom I had met earlier at a women's conference where I was speaking. The evening I met him formally, Brother Koren was among several graduates of Urshan Graduate School of Theology (UGST) who were being recognized at a special event held in their honor. Before the ceremony began, Esther saw me and came by my table to say hello. When I realized her whole family was present, I asked her to introduce me to them all. Esther was my introduction to her father. Can a woman be used similarly to introduce someone else to Jesus? Can she by virtue of her relationship with her heavenly Father teach, exhort, and inspire in word and deed? Does the Bible limit the extent to which a woman can be used? Does the letter of the law take precedence over the spirit of the law?

In penning *He Called Her*, Brother Koren has undertaken the sensitive subject of women in the ministry. He has not come to his conclusions lightly; rather, by his own admission, this book is the culmination of his own personal journey of discovery and discipleship. I admire his honesty in addressing his own preconceptions and appreciate the sincerity and passion with which he has presented his case to three readers: the male minister who wants to lead his congregation according to biblical principles regarding women in ministry; the woman who is seeking understanding about what the call of God might mean to her; and the parishioner who might be in the position to listen to or submit to a woman in ministry.

Brother Koren has invited us as friends to reconsider how we view women in a modern context based on the lives of real women recorded in the Bible and a thorough reexamination of the Scriptures having to do with women in the New

Testament church. He has highlighted examples of biblical women in both the Old and New Testaments who were capable, godly, sincere, and effective leaders. As he aptly notes, from Eve in the Book of Genesis to Jezebel in the Book of Revelation, the Bible simply records the presence of both godly and ungodly women in varying degrees of power and influence and the effects of their leadership or lack thereof. Access to power and authority reveals the person who wields it, male or female, and God can and does use anyone to His own purpose. Being a man in authority does not insure that people will obey; being a woman in authority does not insure that they won't. The test of leadership according to Jesus is the voice of the Shepherd: "And a stranger will they not follow, but will flee from him: for they know not the voice of strangers" (John 10:5). People who know Jesus recognize the sound of His voice regardless of the vessel that speaks. We are all accountable to speak with His voice, no matter what role we occupy.

According to the parable of the vineyard, the Lord is more concerned about the work than who is doing it. Clearly, He has and will continue to exercise His prerogative to use any and everyone, including all of those whom no one else will hire (Matthew 20:6–7). Whatever our individual beliefs about who can and cannot work for the Lord, Brother Koren has challenged us all to lay aside our fears, put our shoulders to the wheel, one and all, and work together as each of us is called and fitted to serve until Jesus comes. The discussion is timely and relevant for all of us who long to serve in our Lord's vineyard.

Preface

Each chapter of this book helps bring clarity for those who have been confused about how to balance a woman's God-given calling with preconceptions some have against women ministers. You might choose to jump through the book reading certain chapters which address your particular concerns. While it is laid out to help you find the topic which interests you, this book also has a continuity that will help lay out the big picture of the role of women in the church. To those who jump around from chapter to chapter, I invite you to come back afterward and read the book through from beginning to end. Reassess any preconceived ideas you have had and let God's Word give you confidence that He has called all His children—both sons and daughters—to join Him in building His kingdom.

The writing of a book like this could probably have not come from a less likely person. As a child wandering up and down the toy aisles, I would have a panic attack if I stumbled into the pink aisle. Terror would grip me at the very thought of walking between those racks of dolls, hula hoops, and other pink-pink, girlie stuff. Partly, I feared being seen by friends who would tease me, and I also stayed on high alert for the dreaded disease of cooties. In adulthood, it has been my joy to parent four young men who also are "all boy." As they roam the woods and learn to work on our eighteen rolling acres, my guys understand the value of denim and camouflage. However, after two decades with my wife and many great memories with my three daughters, I am well acquainted with the pastel regions of life. I must say I am better for it.

Not only did I misunderstand and avoid all things feminine in my childhood, I became an adult and later a preacher who did not approve of women pastors. It cost me nothing to mentally remove women from a role as teacher or preacher. Nothing, that is, but silencing several voices of those who had taught me how to pray and win souls. During my time at Urshan Graduate School of Theology, I chose the topic of women in ministry for my thesis. As I closely examined God's Word, I found my prejudices as well-founded as my childhood fears of the pink aisle.

Ultimately, my discoveries formed this book because the church must hear this message, even though I never dreamed I would focus my efforts in this direction. I believe I can claim to be impartial in my approach to this topic since I am not defending my wife or other close relative's ministry. I simply wish to be faithful to the Word of God and to the calling of God on the lives of whomever He chooses. Through these pages, we will look at the unique Pentecostal perspective on women in ministry and what the Bible clearly says on this topic.

I write for the male minister who wants to be faithful to the word of God and the believers he leads, the woman who needs clarity on what to do with the calling God has given her, and church members who want to know if they should follow a woman in leadership.

Acknowledgements

First, I want to thank the Lord Jesus for giving women a place in His kingdom. I give Him all credit for any skills or insights I have had in writing this book to encourage them in that call. Any errors or flaws in this book would be my own.

Second, I want to thank my incredible wife Leanne for being an example of the bride of Christ. In spite of my piles of books and erratic writing hours, her untiring patience and encouragement throughout this task has been heroic. My Proverbs 31 woman has blessed me with seven wonderful children whom she is raising in truth and love.

Third, I want to thank all those who invested in me through the years. My parents, Roger and Cheryl Koren inspired my love for the Lord and fascination with studying His Word. Paul Howe, my father-in-law, has spoken well of me even when I did not deserve it and has always encouraged me in my calling. David Norris challenged me to pursue a formal education and became one of my favorite instructors in my graduate studies. Carlton Coon Sr. believed in my ministry and encouraged me to write. Many others who taught, prayed for, and invested in me would be too lengthy to list, but I realize the great host of witnesses to whom I am beholden.

Last but most pertinent to this project, I wish to thank the hard-working folks at Word Aflame. Everett Gossard has been an incredibly patient yet professional editor. His attention to detail has honed this project to be more understandable and palatable for your reading. David Bernard's leadership and writing in general coupled with his support of women in ministry has had no small role in influencing the development of this book.

And thank you, dear reader, for taking the time to read a biblical validation for God's calling of women.

1 | *He Called Junia: Women as Missionaries*

Is the idea of women in ministry a new thing?

Greet Andronicus and Junia, my countrymen and my fellow prisoners, who are of note among the apostles, who also were in Christ before me (Romans 16:7).[1]

"We just licensed several new women ministers!" someone told me. Is this good news or bad news? As I heard reports like this, I wondered how we justified having women preachers in spite of what the Bible seemed to say against women's roles within the church. Yet, no one mentioned such a concern, gladly giving bravos and backslapping to the aspiring female ministers. I felt ill at ease with the idea that we were disregarding what the Word of God said. When I spoke to friends in ministry about my concerns, I did not hear any satisfying answers.

Everything a child of God does has to line up with Scripture. If the Bible speaks against something, I do not want to be a part of it. Since this issue regarding women in

> *I wondered how we justified having women preachers in spite of what the Bible seemed to say against women's roles within the church.*

ministry did not concern me personally, I did not feel compelled to study it. I saw it as an issue for someone else to resolve.

While studying Romans, I encountered women ministers. Junia is one of them. This woman was an apostle. The sound of "woman apostle" may be startling. Many church groups do not use the word apostle with reference to people living today, much less to a woman. An apostle is one "sent out" by the Lord as His messenger. Modern missionaries (those "sent abroad") are apostles for distant lands, bringing the message of the gospel and establishing churches.

Paul mentioned a few women in significant ministry roles. I wonder if he ever imagined such brief references could become the fodder for whole chapters and even whole books. It seems that "women in ministry" was not such a novelty by his time. The way he briefly mentions Junia and moves on indicates that this was not such a new thing, at least for the believers in Rome. Christianity was such a fast-growing movement that everything was a new normal all at the same time. Although women in leadership may have been socially shocking in Jesus' time, it appears a woman minister was understood as normal by the time Paul wrote his epistles.

When I first objected to women in ministry, I thought of male ministry roles as being normative. For example, under Moses, only men could be priests.[2] In response, however, one could state that, "if we restrict ministry to men because priests were male, why should we not restrict it also to a particular tribe, as the law clearly did?"[3] The logic of saying a minister must be male based on such a precedent might lead to this thinking, too:

> To be consistent, handicapped men would also have to be excluded, as well as male dwarfs, young men and older men, men with skin diseases, single men, men married to a widow or men with a wife who had been raped. *All* Gentiles and *most* Jews would be disqualified! Even those who qualified would be considered much of the time to be physically unclean, and therefore unfit for communion with God.[4]

The priesthood ended with Jesus who is of a new order of priest—God-called.[5] Women can serve of the same order—called by God. Apostles are not just Jewish men. Disciples and missionaries also arise by the high calling of God.

APOSTLES BEYOND THE TWELVE

Apostle Junia was one of those women who found support from men in ministry. She moved out from the margins, pioneered for the faith, and got herself arrested. In spite of the support she got from Paul and Andronicus, she has not always been so well received.

Since many men assumed a woman could not be in leadership, some Bible translations have reflected that bias by using the name "Junias," a masculine name, in the place of "Junia" as it should read. The KJV and many newer versions have correctly translated this verse because, for one thing, we have found no record of a man in first-century culture with the name Junias. Second, it is wrong to change any word of Scripture in order to support one's belief.

Others who disapprove of women in leadership argue that Junia may have been a woman, but she was only "well known to" the apostles. Instead of trying to change her gender, they try to change the meaning of the passage which mentions her. In other words, only the apostles knew who she was, they say, and thought highly of her.[6] Looking at other passages where Paul uses this phrase lets us know that he literally meant they were significant within the group of people called apostles.[7] The statement "of note among the apostles" lets us know that Junia and Andronicus were not just apostles, but exceptional in their calling. Junia did more than just travel with her husband. Apostle Peter had a wife who travelled with him, but she was never referred to as an apostle.

Junia was a leader, not just someone with a title. Many hold a view that the twelve apostles were the only apostles to ever exist. However, this denies the multiple references in Scripture to other apostles beyond the original twelve. Luke used the word apostle differently than Paul did. While Luke reserved the word mainly for the Twelve who had been there from the beginning of Jesus' ministry, Paul mentioned several leaders as being apostles.

For over four decades, Janice Alvear has been an apostle to Brazil. She describes what being a missionary means:

> Well for me, it has meant going into the cities, the villages, the jungles, and telling a pagan people about the life changing story of Jesus Christ. It has meant being challenged by witch doctors and priests, being threatened by bandits, standing before cannibal Indians, working in a leper colony as well as speaking in public schools and universities of Brazil.
>
> It meant going into places where male preachers had never been allowed but some condemned me for being willing to go. I had to wade across alligator-infested streams just to reach and baptize new converts. Being a missionary meant performing weddings, burying the dead and sometimes delivering babies.
>
> It meant teaching new converts and preparing people for the ministry. It meant seeing a work be born and grow into maturity. It meant hours of radio programs. It meant long nights without sleep, traveling in the back lands, drinking contaminated water and eating all kinds of so called foods (some of which were indescribable). It meant sharing rooms with bats, rats, and all sorts of animals that crawled and flew at night.
>
> It meant sitting in the conventions in the homeland and listening to men who made cutting remarks about women in the ministry. It meant being willing to go against the tide and obey a call that is stronger than meager earthly ties. It meant being different from the ordinary. It meant loving souls, no matter the circumstances. It meant taking in abandoned children whose mother was murdered because she herself was a preacher of the Name of Jesus, then adopting them and loving them like my own.

> . . . Perhaps most prophets and prophetesses in the Bible had to travel down lonely roads themselves to obey God yet they could not understand why at that moment. I, too, am at a loss for words to describe the desolate anguish I had experienced at times. Equally difficult to explain is the call of God so strong in my heart. Maybe it's all part of being a missionary. How can you describe a feeling too deep for words, a call too sacred to play around with? This burden is so heavy that it never disappears.[8]

An apostle serves on the frontlines, fighting spiritual strongholds and developing leaders.

Paul recognized Junia as one of those who had faced jail time for the sake of the gospel. It would hardly be likely that a woman would face arrest in that era without having done something significant to provoke the ire of the authorities.[9] Typical women blended into the social fabric. This woman must have been quite outspoken even for a woman preacher. Did she preach in the city streets, lead a school of Christian evangelists, or confront a religious leader publicly as the other apostles had been arrested for? We do not know, but we do know she earned her title. Early translations of Scripture and early commentators on the writings of Paul affirm that he was addressing a female apostle.[10] Ancient Greek speakers such as Origen and Chrysostom understood Paul to mean she was a true apostle, as well.[11] Some scholars suggest that since Andronicus and Junia were in Christ before Paul, they may have been some of the original disciples who followed Jesus in Palestine.[12]

Paul referred to an apostle as someone who has seen Christ;[13] so when he wrote about Junia in Romans 16 he probably had the same idea in mind. Some believe the Greek name Junia in Romans 16:7 may refer to the disciple with the Hebrew name of Joanna in Luke 8:3.[14] If this is so, then Jesus began the line of women ministers.[15] Joanna

An apostle serves on the frontlines, fighting spiritual strongholds and developing leaders.

was a chief supporter of Jesus' ministry; Junia was an apostle who had born fruit as a missionary. Joanna, along with other women, was one of the first to *preach* the message of Jesus' resurrection.[16] Either way, whether these names represent one woman or two, we see the Lord's inclusion of women and the apostle Paul's recognition of that call as well.[17]

An apostle is a gift from the Lord: "He Himself gave some to be apostles, some prophets, some evangelists, and some pastors and teachers" (Ephesians 4:11). If anything, I do not want to reject the ministry of a God-called woman because that would be rejecting a gift from the Lord Himself. Paul consistently placed apostles at the top of the list of ministry callings: "God has appointed these in the church: first apostles, second prophets, third teachers, after that miracles, then gifts of healings, helps, administrations, varieties of tongues" (I Corinthians 12:28). How refreshing to find Junia here, demonstrating that women can serve in whatever capacity to which the Lord calls them. An apostle/missionary trains and appoints pastors, teachers, prophets, and evangelists. Even today, women of God walk in the role of apostle to countries and cities around the world.

WOMEN IN REVIVAL MOVEMENTS

Women serve a crucial part in God's plan for revival. Revival is more than just a series of services scheduled at a church. In revival, the Spirit moves in such a way as to draw hearts, work miracles, and deliver hundreds and thousands who had been held captive to the enemy.

When Pentecostal revival broke out in Colombia, the missionary recorded this about a young woman named Eucaris who let the Lord use her:

> Eucaris had never felt such a spirit of evangelism. She recited all she had seen happen in Cali and preached a down-to-earth message on the love of God and the need to repent. As she told simple stories, the folks came

under tremendous conviction. Some were weeping; many were getting right with God. Eucaris wept with them, praying earnestly for God to baptize them with His Spirit.

At that moment Saul came in with a bang. Startled, Eucaris took in the situation and prayed that God would stop Saul from ruining the meeting.

Saul couldn't move. He stood transfixed at the door, dazed and confused. It was like he was in a dream; nothing would move, not an arm, not a finger, not an eyelid. . . . [Eucaris] put her hands on his head, and he felt fire go through him as she said, "You need Jesus."

At that moment, released from the force that held him, he dropped to his knees. He could do no more. All he wanted to do was cry and confess and be free from the horror of his condition, to find the beauty he perceived about him. Saul stayed there a long time. When he did get up, the first thing he did was to go back to his bar and pour all his liquor down the mountainside. He was through with it. Forever.[18]

May every church be caught up in a spirit of unending revival like that.

Protestant religious experience cut its teeth with female ministers in the West. Not that they were very accepted at first. In 1636, Anne Hutchinson defended her belief in salvation by faith and an inner witness of the Spirit. Men told her, "You have stept out of your place."[19] Margaret Fell became an early convert to the Quakers and the home she shared with her husband became the organizational center of the movement. She preached and wrote valiantly for the Quaker cause.[20]

In particular, the Holiness movement grew up with women in ministry. Susanna Wesley taught the Bible to her children and soon dozens had gathered to hear her speak. She said, "Though I am not a man, nor a Minister. . . , I might do somewhat more than I do."[21] Soon, she had two hundred people in attendance that she never campaigned for but dared never to turn away. Most only remember her for training up John Wesley, founder of a holiness movement which paved the way for the Pentecostal outpouring.[22]

God-authored revivals reset all kinds of religious norms in a culture. In a revival, the social underdogs and outcasts could do something of significance under the mighty hand of God. The Great Awakening allowed many women to do things for God in public, so much so that men in religious authority protested.

> *God-authored revivals reset all kinds of religious norms in a culture.*

Cynics of the effects brought by the early revivals complained that even women and girls had "taken upon them to do the Business of Preachers."[23] Nevertheless, many respected the input of female preachers, especially those converted under the sound of their voices.

WOMEN SHAPED RELIGIOUS HISTORY

During the Second Great Awakening, a woman could be involved in teaching the children in the home, leading Sunday school classes, organizing benevolent activities, or being a full-time missionary.[24] The role of minister's wife became a highly sought after position for many young women, who then tended to visitation and other pastoral duties.[25] Into the mid-1800s, Ellen Ranyard employed many women in charitable causes such as visiting the poor, selling Bibles, offering nursing care, and providing spiritual counsel.[26]

In this Victorian era, one publication explained the work of women missionaries this way: "Christian civilization does little for a nation until it has lifted woman from the condition of a thing to the dignity of a sister and a wife. You cannot evangelize a country until you convert the women."[27] In general, the women involved in missions were not following feminist ideals. In fact, Marjorie King said, "Missionary women exported femininity, not feminism."[28]

The consistent, historical reason women got involved in ministry was the spirit of revival. Revivals were unquestionably the hand of God, and few dared argue with it even when the Lord worked through a woman. At the end of the eighteenth century, Jarena Lee proved to be a powerful African American preacher. She spoke with a "clarity and reverence seldom heard in those circles" and, although she was not permitted to be ordained, "God's power and spirit had been poured out on her."[29]

Revival reports from 1858 America stirred interest among many in South Africa. In one meeting, after several had offered either a hymn or a prayer, a Fingo girl who served a local farmer received halting permission to rise and pray. While she prayed, "a roll of noise like that of approaching thunder was heard, coming closer and closer until it enveloped the hall, shaking the place."[30] Prayer erupted spontaneously across the group as the Spirit moved in. Andrew Murray found this uproar alarming upon his later arrival and attempted to silence the crowd. His efforts failed as each one "seemed more concerned with calling on God for forgiveness of an intolerable weight of sin and shame."[31] His domineering spirit contrasted against her humble spirit demonstrates the difference between dead religion and revival.

Revival launched many women into ministry at the beginning of the twentieth century. In 1896, Charles Parham bestowed the title of "Reverend Sarah Parham" on his newlywed bride who served with him as assistant pastor into the new century.[32] Hattie Duncan hosted the Elim Faith Home with her sister in 1907.[33] At the age of thirty-one, Alma White responded to a call to preach that she had received when she was sixteen, and went on to start her own holiness movement in the early 1900s. She found disdain in the eyes of her Methodist contemporaries for too much display of emotion and for preaching the possibility of healing.[34]

On Azusa Street in Los Angeles in a mostly black mission, women such as Jennie Moore, Lucy Farrow, and Clara Lum responded to the call as the Pentecostal movement began.[35] Florence Crawford took the message of Pentecost into the Northwest. Marie Burgess carried the message east to New York City where she built a flourishing bastion for Pentecost on Forty-Second Street.[36] Nettie Moomau left her mission work in China to visit Azusa Street in 1906. She brought the message back to the Chinese people and saw revival sweep the country, starting works in almost a dozen cities.[37]

Pandita Ramabai stirred up revival in India at the beginning of the twentieth century and founded a salvation mission for destitute girls. She experienced and embraced an Azusa-type revival and sought to spread revival throughout western India.[38] Influential women within the black church included Henrietta Vinton Davis, M. L. T. De Mena, Amy Jacques Garvey, and Laura Kofey.[39] Hélène Biolley led the founding of the Pentecostal movement in France, building a church of three hundred after miraculous healings softened the hearts of the staunch Catholic population in Le Havre.[40]

Revival knows no race, creed, denomination, or gender. Pentecostalism opened the doors to women in leadership because of its emphasis on a *calling* to ministry, confirming signs seen by the believing community, and the recognition of Joel's latter rain outpouring which included both sons and daughters who would prophesy.[41]

WOMEN IN PENTECOSTAL HISTORY

Just because more women today are answering the call to preach does not mean it is a new thing. Women were key to the work of God in the early church and we find them mentioned everywhere. During the throes of revival harvest, every worker, no matter race or gender, finds a place to stay busy. Perhaps it is the urgent nature of a new movement that causes it to assimilate women quickly and with little question.

Historically, women have always had a place in ministry when God was at work. The early leader of the Quakers encouraged and defended women's ministry to others. George Fox was unknowingly paving the way for future women preachers in Pentecost. Over 40 percent of the Quaker missionaries were women, many of whom were not accompanied by husbands.[42]

The earliest Oneness Pentecostal ministerial directory shows that 29 percent of the ministers were female.[43] One-third of ministers in the Assemblies of God in 1914 were female as well as two-thirds of their missionaries.[44] Perhaps the involvement of women and children in early Pentecost helped upset the religious norms and break loose dead-end traditions. Once the movement matured, did the Lord intend for women to sit down and not serve any longer? That appears to be a historical trend in many movements.

The mentality which demeaned women still seemed to prevail even to some extent in Pentecostal circles. Oma Ellis, a powerful Pentecostal preacher, tells of an experience when she was in desperate need of money and how she felt her being a woman caused the male pastor to treat her differently:

> He explained to the congregation, "I'm going to do something that I would not dare to do to any other evangelist I know. But knowing Sister Oma as I do, I don't believe she will get mad at me. We have a payment due on the church that must be met this week, so I'm not going to give her the offering this evening. Wife and I will see to it that she and her children have food and a place to stay."
>
> I was shocked. "No, he would not dare to treat a man evangelist that way," I thought. I could feel resentment rising in me like angry floodwaters. "Are women's financial needs less important than the needs of men?" . . .
>
> Quickly I prayed, "Lord, please forgive me for this resentment and bitterness and take it away. I am Your servant, and You are aware of my needs. I place them in Your hands." To stand before a congregation stripped

> of the anointing was an embarrassment I did not want to experience.
>
> As I stepped to the pulpit, God's Spirit stepped there with me. Never had I felt any stronger anointing of the Holy Ghost than I did that night. The altar service was good with several souls filled with the Spirit . . . souls that may not have found God if I had not been in touch with Him that night.[45]

After Oma finished preaching, a gentleman approached her and gave her an offering for much more than what she would have expected as a love offering from the church. She reported the offering to the pastor, and he apologized for the way he mishandled the situation. I find it interesting that even though this man was in favor of a woman preacher, he found himself treating her differently than he would have any other preacher.

Though it may be true that women often are active leaders in the beginning of a fresh outpouring of the Lord, it is most likely the nature of humans that edges women out, not the nature of heaven. Pentecost came to many who did not have much status in life. The call of God changed their lives, gave them purpose, and united these dissimilar people. It appears that many groups on the margins of society (the not-so-cool crowd, the outcasts) are initially open to women sharing leadership roles with men. Female religious leadership rarely lasts into the next phase of organization.[46] Even though Pentecostal denominations continued to allow women in ministry, they began to be encouraged to be missionaries or evangelists rather than pastors.[47] Afterward, "as routinization and regimentation of community relationships sets in, a reaction takes place against" even the Spirit-led women, "who come to be regarded as dishonorable."[48] Look through history and you will find that women's leadership does not often continue much longer after the beginning of a religious community. At the beginning, where everyone values spiritual gifts, the God-approved involvement of women is welcomed.

ARE WE STILL IN REVIVAL?

Although this book will help bring clarity to some confusion that has developed in people's minds regarding women preachers, we need to reconnect with our roots. We need church services and evangelistic campaigns where God shows up in such a way that no one cares who has the microphone because the Lord is orchestrating the work. While you examine the many Scriptures that speak to the concept of women in ministry, I pray you would remember that everything can be argued endlessly, but revival will provide more answers than any debate.

When the fervor of a revival movement slows down and participants look to make it a formal organization, those involved tend to look everything over with a critical eye. The historical trend shows that during such a phase, the women who once were central to the life of the movement begin to be moved back to the fringe of the community.

> *Revival will provide more answers than any debate.*

By the second century, after several women had made great progress for the Kingdom (and the reputation of their gender), we find the inevitable backlash at work. David Bernard mentions that "as the church became more institutionalized and formalized, it began to lose its emphasis on spiritual gifts and the priesthood of all believers. . . . Since the ministry of women was closely connected to, and justified by, the anointing of the Spirit rather than cultural norms, when charismatic ministry declined and disappeared so did the ministry of women."[49] The question lingers as to whether the rejection of women in ministry causes revival to fade or if the death of revival causes a reversion to old prejudices. What if by allowing women a place to answer God's call on their lives we will experience true and lasting revival?

Even revival movements in recent history quickly recovered from the novelty of women leaders and were quick to return to social norms. The revivals which came and went throughout the nineteenth century began to reflect this trend of negativism toward women in ministry. Somehow the tables turned around the mid-twentieth century when more theologically liberal, mainline denominations began ordaining women. Although this appeared to be a win for women in ministry, by the late twentieth century, percentages of women preachers in conservative denominations had declined.[50]

As the era of revivals waned, there arose a crusade to correct the statistical "problem" of the churches having twice as many women as men. This campaign, called the "Men and Religion Forward Movement," attempted to "correct" a perceived shortage of nearly three million men from churches. This imbalance had existed since the 1660s, but this campaign marked the first concerted attempt to impose a balance of the genders.[51]

Although women's charities and missions carried much influence, the all-male general assembly in one denomination disbanded the women's boards and merged them with several men's groups. In the mixed-sex boards, women received only about a third of the seats and in other denominations the male leaders arbitrarily used the funds the ladies' ministries had collected.[52]

While the men's campaign brought a resurgence of men into the churches, it appears to have negatively affected mainline denominations, and as the men "disbanded women's organizations; women church leaders lost their authority."[53] No doubt the men's slogan of "the women have had charge of the church work long enough" must have justified the upset in religious control.[54] It is no surprise that women soon flocked to the business world to find their identity and grasp at some purpose beyond the home. Christians have been accused from within that "when we get our eyes on churches [and] creedism, [...] we elbow the women preachers off."[55]

Many men have gone out of their way to involve women in ministry. Charles Finney included women in his new measures for promoting revivals in the Second Great Awakening. The success of his revivals plowed the way forward for female religious leadership. He also heavily involved women in behind-the-scenes preparation for revival—most importantly intercessory prayer meetings.[56] Organized efforts to teach and pray over children helped mothers understand what to do for their flock at home, including praying and fasting for each child on his or her birthday. Years later, many men were transformed as revival brought them to their knees and they remembered their mother praying for them and teaching them the ways of the Lord. Arguably, revivals would never have reached the proportions they did if the foundation of faith had not already been in place.[57] Preachers or not, women who ministered as mothers laid the bedrock of many revivals.

I cannot imagine anyone arguing against women influencing their children in the ways of the Lord. However, should women speak in such revivals? Could a woman be the evangelist at a camp meeting? The next chapter will examine that thought.

2 | He Called Mary: Women as Evangelists

Can a woman preach the gospel?

> *Now it happened as they went that He entered a certain village; and a certain woman named Martha welcomed Him into her house. And she had a sister called Mary, who also sat at Jesus' feet and heard His word.*
> *But Martha was distracted with much serving, and she approached Him and said, "Lord, do You not care that my sister has left me to serve alone? Therefore tell her to help me."*
> *And Jesus answered and said to her, "Martha, Martha, you are worried and troubled about many things. But one thing is needed, and Mary has chosen that good part, which will not be taken away from her"*
> *(Luke 10:38–42).*

The story of Jesus endorsing Mary's participation as a disciple might have been as culturally shocking then as a Jew eating a ham sandwich. In a culture where men prayed, "Thank you Lord that I am not a slave, a dog, or a woman," Jesus welcomed Mary into His ministry team. Jesus used women as positive illustrations of the kingdom of God.[1] Not only did women listen to His speeches on the hillside in Bethany, Jesus included them in the inner group He was training for ministry.

Having a woman sit at the feet of a Rabbi could have been as scandalous as any other anti-traditional thing Jesus did. After having this socially unacceptable situation pointed out, Jesus could have played it down by saying, "Look, she's only listening not teaching," or "Okay, Mary, you can listen but not teach anyone else what I am saying," or even "Wow, I better not let this go too far." Instead, He gave her the same freedom to learn as the men in the room and applauded her choice over what was typically considered the woman's place.

Proud Judas thought he could tell the woman how to worship. Mary came and washed Jesus' feet, wiped them with her hair, and anointed Him with a beautiful aroma. Judas scorned her contribution. Jesus defended her true worship. He saw to it that such an act of sacrifice by a woman would be spoken of everywhere His story was told. I cannot think of much I have done that would fit right alongside the gospel message. Mary's story does.

Mary followed the Lord with deep love for Him after He rescued her from so much.[2] He raised her brother from the dead. Many things had brought her to a profound faith in the Lord. She could see He was the long awaited Messiah.

Perhaps that is why she had such a hard time grappling with His death when it occurred. At the empty tomb, the angels told her and the others to go share the good news with the disciples. Afterward, frustrated and confused, Mary sank into a heap in the garden. She railed against a gardener as if he were to blame for what had happened.

He called, "Mary," and her heart melted.

The fears turned to tears as she realized He still called her by name. It was Jesus. She shouted, "My Teacher!"

Jesus then sent her as a messenger for Him. She would represent Him to the others to share a message of hope with them. When He said, "Go and tell My brethren," she was officially commissioned to preach the news of His resurrection.

Janice Sjostrand points out key meanings from the life of Mary:

> She had clung to Jesus in life; she would cling to Him in death. . . . A tormented woman, once possessed by evil, waited for her Christ at His cross and tomb and became His first messenger. . . . Oh that Mary's example from the past would resonate with us. She never walked away. She kept waiting for something to happen, and it did! May we all persevere because of love, because of what Jesus has already done, because of hope, until He appears with a personal response for each of us, and a word for our brethren."[3]

Instead of getting in trouble for declaring truth to men, Mary received confirmation that she must deliver a message from the Lord![4]

JESUS' FEMALE DISCIPLES

Mary was one of many disciples in addition to the original twelve. Jesus' calling of the Twelve had meaning beyond their immediate experience. In the New Jerusalem, their names join the names of the twelve tribes in majestic symbolism of the new household of faith.[5] Jesus told these men, "You who have followed Me will also sit on twelve thrones, judging the twelve tribes of Israel."[6] However, this does not imply that all preachers need to be male (or from Galilee or even of Jewish decent).

> It was not inconsistent for Jesus to be countercultural in some ways (allowing women disciples) but to accommodate his culture in others (choosing males for the Twelve, whom he would send out to evangelize). Ministry in any culture

"Ministry in any culture requires decisions on which priorities we must fight for."
– Craig Keener

> requires decisions on which priorities we must fight for. . . . For practical reasons, Jesus also chose no Gentiles (impossible) and possibly no Judeans (for geographic reasons).[7]

Looking at this situation through another cultural lens might help. In my youth, my parents served for a summer on a mission field. One day I wanted to join the Bible school students who were going out to invite locals to church, but in this racially oppressed environment I felt the brunt of reality. The outreach leader said, "You can't go. If most of them saw a white man at their door, they would not come to our church." God wanted to use me and I wanted to go, but the local scenario would not allow it. I can see something similar here in Jesus' selecting of the disciples as well, although gender and racial issues obviously have different tensions and dynamics.

Some say that if Jesus was so in favor of women in ministry, He would have given them official roles. By the same reasoning, He was pro-slaves, pro-Gentiles, and pro-underdogs of every stripe, but He made none of them part of His twelve. We should not make a point from a story that the author did not intend for the original audience.

Several women traveled with Jesus and supported Him out of their own finances (Luke 8:3). "The inclusion of women among Jesus' traveling coterie shows they were permitted to make the same radical commitment in following Jesus as the Twelve and others did."[8] It would be anti-missional of Jesus to reject women.[9] He came to include all: whosoever would come. He specifically made the point that He would do like Elijah and choose a Gentile woman over a self-righteous Israelite.[10]

> The sages ruled that women were not to be appointed as officials, and we never read of rabbis ordaining women disciples to be rabbis. We know of one rabbi who

followed a different practice: Jesus had women a his disciples (Luke 10:39; cf. 8:1–3; Mark 15:4' chose them as witnesses of his resurrection (M 28:1–10; Luke 24:1–11; John 20:10–18).[11]

In a culture that suppressed women, Jesus used women as illustrations in His parables.[12]

During a time when women were so subjugated that a man could divorce his wife if she left the house with her head uncovered, it was revolutionary to reveal spiritual truths through a woman's behavior! The historian Jeremias said, "Only against the background of that time can we fully appreciate Jesus's attitude to women."[13] The number of women following Jesus[14]

> was an unprecedented happening in the history of that time. John the Baptist had already preached to women (Matthew 21:32) and baptized them; Jesus, too, knowingly overthrew custom when he allowed women to follow him. He could do this because he required from his disciples an attitude [toward] women of complete chastity [See Matthew 5:28.] Jesus was not content with bringing women up onto a higher plane than was then the custom; but as Saviour of all (Luke 7:36–50), he brings them before God on an equal footing with men (Matthew 21:31-32).[15]

It is not by accident we find the stories about women in the gospels. How the Lord treated them was part of His message.[16]

Jesus' treatment of women was not that radical in comparison to the rest of the Bible. Women had participated in worship back in the Old Covenant: Miriam led in song, women served before the Tent of the Lord, and Anna gave her years after marriage to the Temple.[17] It was not a new thing for women to be part of the faith. Jesus' attitude toward women upended the cultural setting in which He lived.

When Jesus' identity was revealed to Peter who cried out, "You are the Christ of God," He told his disciples about His resurrection. Some of those close disciples were women. We can infer this because the angels in the tomb said, "Remember how He spoke to you when He was still in Galilee, saying, 'The Son of Man must be delivered into the hands of sinful men, and be crucified, and the third day rise again.'" Comparing this verse in Luke 24:6–7 with 9:22 we see that women heard the original statement from Jesus. The angels recognized these women as close disciples whom Jesus told about His future plans.

Luke and Acts, both penned by the same writer, mention women thirty-three times in each book. Luke's song of Mary, the mother of our Lord, presents her as a theologian and spokesperson for what God is doing, in Luke 1:46–56.[18] No one can read the Gospel of Luke without observing the prominence of her contribution. The Book of Acts overtly focuses on the battle for Gentile inclusion in the church, and subtly moves the mission forward to include women in ministry as well.[19]

WOMEN PROCLAIMING GOOD NEWS TO MEN

All four of the gospels describe the resurrection story from a different angle and with different emphasis, but each version makes it clear that women were the first to believe and the first to speak the message of hope.[20] Not only did they speak, but they preached to men. The men thought the women's words were "idle tales, and they did not believe them"![21] Instead of going to Galilee, Peter ran to the tomb to see for himself.

Mary and the other women did not just announce what had happened, but told the men what to do. Jesus told the believing women, "Go and tell My brethren to go to Galilee" (Matthew 28:10). Under instructions from the Lord himself, the women preached to the men what they were to do next.

Similarly, God called Howard Goss's wife of his youth to be a fiery evangelist:

> Millicent had started preaching about the same time I had received the Baptism, and God mightily used her as an evangelist, her special gift. Our workers called her "Little David" because of her remarkable preaching ability, her beautiful alto voice, and because one of her best sermons was about the meeting of David and Goliath. God used her mightily here in Austin, as she did most of the night preaching.[22]

Even today, a little woman can bring tough men to weeping repentance under the anointing of the Holy Ghost.

We see women in Scripture commissioned to inform and instruct. Neither the angels nor the risen Lord seemed troubled at sending the women to deliver an authoritative message to men hiding behind locked doors. God uses women to speak for Him.

"Who are you to judge another's servant? To his own master he stands or falls. Indeed, he will be made to stand, for God is able to make him stand" (Romans 14:4). I am still confident in God to do great things through those He calls. Of course, those He calls to serve Him need training and supervision. Yes, a servant of God must be submitted to another servant of God. However, nothing says that a God-called worker has to be a male.

In Jewish culture, men stood at the center of everything religious. At the resurrection scene, however, they are on the fringes, away from the action, hiding upstairs, yet the women are at the center, not just entering the tomb, but hearing from heaven *for the men*! Think about the humor in the idea of fearful men listening to the bold message of Mary. She was not the last woman to speak for the Lord, either.

In the revivals of previous centuries, hundreds of women served as evangelists and preachers. Many denominations ordained women preachers.[23] The Holiness movement welcomed women in leadership because "the work of the Holy Spirit in sanctification was a more important qualification than formal education for preaching the gospel."[24]

In the eighteenth century, Mary Fletcher would preach on the steps leading to the pulpit for fear of appearing too masculine when preaching. She would "expound" on a chapter of the Bible rather than "speak from a text" as that would seem too much like a sermon. A close friend of John Wesley, she found his favor as he became more accepting of women preachers. Wesley had warmed to the idea of women preachers from his youth while watching his mother nurture many (in contrast to his father's riotous attempts at ministry). Wesley told Fletcher, "I think the strength of the cause rests there—on your having an *extraordinary* call."[25] Mary preached to crowds of three thousand, including many ministers. Complaints against her ministry on account of her gender were often settled by Wesley, others, or God Himself. One man tried to take the stand in her place, but when he got to the pulpit, his words stopped and his mind went blank. He never opposed her again.[26]

> *I think the strength of the cause rests . . . on your having an extraordinary call.*
> *– John Wesley*

In the nineteenth century, Hannah Whitall Smith preached to a convention in Britain of seven thousand ministers and laypeople from many different countries.[27] Mary Buck became a popular preacher attracting large crowds. Charles Spurgeon trained "Bible women" who served as local evangelists. Fanny Guinness decried ministers who proved "useless or worse than useless in the work of soul saving and preach for years without being instrumental in a single conversion."[28]

One woman preacher, Geraldine Hooper, fought much resistance in her traditional denomination, but when revival began "the people came out in crowds, and the place was filled" and her words came as "kindling a fresh flame."[29] In the Holiness movement, men seemed to have "little difficulty in accepting guidance and exhortation from the women who were often its chief exponents."[30] Women also responded quickly, as did Matilda Bass, who had once been opposed to women in ministry. She changed her views upon hearing the preaching of Miss Hooper and became a preacher as well. Maria Woodworth-Etter drew crowds of over eight thousand as a holiness preacher who discovered Pentecost at the age of sixty-eight.[31]

THE PREACHER IN SYCHAR

The first record we have of a female evangelist is the woman at the well.[32] I just wonder what the mostly male readers thought when they read John's statement that several "believed in Him because of the word of the woman who testified" (John 4:39). In a society that kept women out of the courtroom and silenced them in the synagogue, the Lord commissioned women preachers.

In John's day, this woman at the well was the unlikeliest of leaders. Her story contrasts with Nicodemus's story which preceded hers. Notice the differences in the private meeting with the woman at the well and the man who came secretly to Jesus. The man was the ideal person, for John's readership, while the woman would have been socially despised. Consider:

> Nicodemus was named — the woman was unnamed
> he was male — she was female
> he was a Jew — she was a Jewish outcast
> he met Jesus in the dark — she met Him in broad daylight
> he was respected by his community — she was shunned
> he was socially flawless — she had failed relationships
> he was ritually clean — she was unclean by Jewish law
> he did not commit himself — she committed to Jesus
> he saw Jesus as a teacher — she realized He was Messiah
> he brought no one — she brought the town to Him
> he just walked away — she ran with the mission[33]

John contrasted these stories to make a statement about a woman being able to recognize the truth and share it with others.

To Jesus, women were as capable as men in their ability to grasp theological truth.[34] Evidence of this comes when one reads the full story in John 4 where Jesus has a longer dialogue with this woman about spiritual things than he has with any man in any of the gospels. Not only did she hear and understand, but she turned around and preached the message. Both the Gospel of Luke and the Book of Acts, by the same author, demonstrate that Jesus brought those on the fringes of society to the center—women were part of that emphasis.

If women realized their inclusion in the calling, they might have the boldness of the Samaritan woman. Nona Freeman told how she fouled up her first attempt at speaking for the Lord:

> After Mom asked me to preach, three other preachers came. I begged her to let one of them take my place.
>
> She remained adamant, "Sis, it is time for you to obey the Lord."
>
> The Lord had graciously given me a message, but I preceded it with a long apology, "I am not a preacher and never will be one…" and on and on I went. By that time I had lost the message. I talked a few moments and turned the service back to Mother. She preached with great anointing and after the altar call and some necessary socializing she found me in the kitchen crying.
>
> "Sis, did you believe that God knows what He is doing?"
>
> "Well, I think He has made a mistake this time," I muttered.
>
> "Young lady, He never has made a mistake, and never will. You stop apologizing for Him. If you had gone ahead and given your message, He would have anointed you and it would have been blessed. Let me give you some good ideas. Skip the introduction and the get acquainted speech. Just get up and read the scripture God gave you and PREACH—when inspiration lifts,

you shut up and sit down." After more than sixty-five years—I'm still trying to follow my mother's advice. It seems to work.[35]

RESPONDING TO THE FEMALE VOICE

While driving one day, I was mulling over the different arguments regarding women in ministry when the GPS voice interrupted my thoughts telling me where to turn next. Suddenly I was convicted of my imbalanced values. If I could take directions from a computer-generated female voice and follow her step-by-step instructions, why would I have a problem with a female voice showing me the path to take spiritually?

Can a woman only give direction to other women? Apparently not. How many more souls would discover the empty tomb and meet the risen Lord if more women were encouraged to declare the good news? I remember watching DVDs from a ladies conference and being in awe of the great insights given by the woman preacher. While telling another minister some of the principles I had learned, he mentioned that he had watched those messages, too. Suddenly the silliness of the situation struck me. I wondered how many other women-shouldn't-preach-to-men kind of guys were hiding at home watching some great preaching from anointed women of the Lord.

The Spirit of God that speaks through a man is the same Spirit that will work through a woman. While women often minister in a women-only setting, there is no such thing as a feminine or a masculine anointing. We serve one Lord. The anointing from God through a woman can touch every life, not just female lives.

> *There is no such thing as a feminine or a masculine anointing; we serve one Lord.*

We should see more Marys preaching with resurrection power at local and regional church meetings. If women were chosen to relay the most important message to the Lord's hand-picked men, we should encourage them to do the same now. Regardless what any of us have been told about the role of women in the church, we must recognize the role the Lord gives them.

It appears that many believers accept the idea of a woman sharing the gospel. In the past, women ministers found the most acceptance by taking the gospel to mission fields and areas that had not heard a preacher. Paul even had to go to the societal fringes when the Jews would reject him. The fact that women have had to work the edges of the field in ministry is not just because they are women but also because of the nature of the mission. Not many noble or wise but those on the fringes come to faith.[36]

How can we give room for more women to preach when we see Bible verses that appear to forbid such actions? The next chapter begins to examine this.

3 | He Called Anna: Women as Prophets

Does I Corinthians 14:34–35 silence women in church?

> *Now there was one, Anna, a prophetess, the daughter of Phanuel, of the tribe of Asher. She was of a great age, and had lived with a husband seven years from her virginity; and this woman was a widow of about eighty-four years, who did not depart from the temple, but served God with fastings and prayers night and day. And coming in that instant she gave thanks to the Lord, and spoke of Him to all those who looked for redemption in Jerusalem (Luke 2:36–38).*

Initially I did not get personally involved in the women-in-ministry discussion. Since I did not have any close relatives or even women in the local church wanting to preach, I did not feel I had to find an answer to this dilemma. Then, reality hit.

While teaching the stories of the kings of Judah I encountered Huldah. King Josiah needed to hear from God and sent for her to see what the Lord had to say. Why did he seek out a woman instead of Zephaniah or Jeremiah? The more I prepared to teach that lesson, the more conflicting I found the discussion. On one hand, I found passages of Scripture which appeared to be saying women could not speak or minister to the church, and on the other I found the Lord saying He wanted the daughters to prophesy (Joel 2:28–29).

After studying this topic for a couple days, I remember calling an elder on that Wednesday morning. I unloaded on him my crisis of faith: the Bible was not consistent. God worked through women and spoke through them, but in other passages it appeared He restricted them from speaking (which this book will discuss). I thank God for a godly mentor who strengthened my faith in God and His Word. Though I did not find all the answers I sought at that point, I was able to get up and teach a lesson titled, "Prophetess or Profitless." I anchored my message on Joel's prophecy that God would pour out His Spirit on everyone and He was calling daughters and handmaids to speak for Him. This passage is foundational to the Pentecostal experience as Peter demonstrated in Acts 2, at the grand opening of the New Testament church.

> *Sons and daughters, male and female servants shall prophesy.*

In my zeal to defend Scripture verses that were apparently contradictory, I attempted to cover all of the verses that applied to women in ministry. One that seemed to strike the hardest said "if they want to learn something, let them ask their own husbands at home; for it is shameful for women to speak in church" (I Corinthians 14:34). I remember facing a disturbance where two women kept talking while I was trying to teach. *Aha!* I thought, *this is why this passage is here—for these kinds of women.*

Then reality struck: neither one had a believing husband. This verse did not apply to them at all. How could they learn anything about the things of God, not having a husband who could answer their questions? While my trust in God on this topic had been rightfully reinforced by my mentor, my misunderstanding of this passage still left me confused. If women were to ask questions and learn at home, why even come to church?

People usually skirt around this passage with a few different guesses at what it means. You probably don't want to see I Corinthians 14:34–35 on a banner in the foyer of your church:

> Let your women keep silent in the churches,
> for they are not permitted to speak;
> but they are to be submissive, as the law also says.
> And if they want to learn something,
> let them ask their own husbands at home;
> for it is shameful for women to speak in church.

No matter how you look at it, these verses call for women to stay quiet. While looking at this passage we must be aware of all of God's Word.

ANNA SPOKE UP AT CHURCH

Anna loved the things of God. She was faithful to His house. Her husband had died only seven years into their marriage. Anna devoted herself to the things of God. She did not grow up in Jerusalem but came from the tribe of Asher. This northern tribe did not make big news in a day when those from Judah or Levi claimed so much attention. She spent her time in the Temple praying, fasting, and waiting on the Lord.

Anna, like her namesake Hannah of old, was longing for a child. One day, He came to the Temple in the arms of His mother. When this century-old woman saw the child she had been longing for, she knew He was the One. Jewish women were not allowed to speak up in the synagogue. They had to be quiet and not talk about the Scriptures with the male rabbis and scholars. What was Anna to do? Here was the salvation of humanity before her eyes. She thanked the Lord—out loud! Then she hurried about telling others in the Temple area how redemption had come to Israel. She spoke, and the Book of Luke applauds her devotion and zeal in telling others.

Anna did not worry about not being allowed to talk. She was going to tell others about her Savior, starting at the House of the Lord. She was doing what He had called her to do: wait for Him and announce His arrival. If the Lord records her as a godly example, would He want women to be silent about Him today? I believe He would still want them to speak out loud about Him in the congregation.

Malinda Montgomery knew what it was to be chosen by God yet face rejection by those who misunderstood her gender's role in the body of Christ:

> [The] organized body of ministers encouraged Sister Montgomery's ordination, and she served as editor of its official organ, "The True Light Messenger" for a while. They began to grow and some felt that the lady ministers were no longer needed. Their attitude was that the women were all right for getting things started, for making the sacrifices, for helping to hold it together until the men could do it alone, then the women suddenly were not to "speak in the churches." The dissension was quite a blow to her previous efforts. . . .
>
> As she evaded opportunities to preach and made excuses instead of appointments, her health began to fail. She was only forty-five when she became so physically ill that she could not attend the tent revival service only one half block away. This was the first time I could ever remember Mother missing this annual event. Of course, we children did not know the battle she was fighting. . . .
>
> "Oh, God," she prayed. "Help me to know Your will. Show me clearly the right. Please, don't let me be wrong. For what good is a measure of success when purchased with the coins of error?"
>
> In sudden fright, she opened her eyes as a brilliant light flooded the room. A Voice seemed to emanate from the brightness. "Would you obey the call of God, or fear the voice of man? Will you answer to man in judgment, or to your Lord? Men have their calling and their opposition to overcome. You have yours. Offenses will come, but you must do the work of He who saved you in spite of such hostilities." The brightness faded.

"Yes, Lord, I'll work for You in any capacity of Your choosing. Neither will I allow opposition to hinder my obligation to Your Cause ever again." She fell into a peaceful sleep and awoke completely well. Victory![1]

WOMEN CAN SPEAK IN THE CHURCH

Some denominations apply I Corinthians 14:34–35 by simply not allowing women to speak in church services. Pentecostals, however, cannot do this. We immediately see the tension this passage presents because we know the Spirit is for everyone. When God's Spirit moves on a person, the mouth moves: either in tongues or prophecy. This was true of prophetesses in the Old Testament (prophecy) and it is true of God's daughters in the New Testament.

Scripture encourages women in the church to pray out loud, prophesy, and speak in tongues. However, we have a dilemma if we try to apply this mandate of silence. Does this prohibition mean we cannot have women singers? Ladies cannot pray out loud? Our young women cannot speak in tongues? Some leaders may feel conflicted, fearing we are violating commands in God's Word if a sister gives a testimony in church.

To give a sense of how challenging this might be, when considering all the roles in the Kingdom that require one to speak, think of how a woman might see the list of ministry callings from I Corinthians 12:28:

> ~~first apostles,~~
> ~~second prophets,~~
> ~~third teachers,~~
> after that miracles,
> then gifts of healings,
> helps,
> administrations,
> ~~varieties of tongues.~~

Immediately, we should realize that this cannot be the case. Junia was an apostle. Anna was a prophetess. Both had to speak for God. Miriam and Elizabeth not only spoke, but God recorded their words for us to read and memorize!

A prophet comes as God's spokesperson. In the Old Covenant, it wasn't primarily the priest, but the prophet who spoke for God. Nathan, for example, was a prophet who ministered to King David much in the way a pastor would minister today. The question is not whether a woman can serve as priest. The question, if one were looking for parallels to the Old Covenant, would be "Can a woman serve as a prophet?" Both Old and New Testaments say, "Yes!"

Calvinists (sometimes called cessationists) say the office of prophet is not for today.[2] Usually, these same people also say women cannot be in a speaking ministry or leadership role. Pentecostals believe God still calls prophets to speak words of encouragement or correction. While there is a valid discussion of the difference between one who prophesies and one who is called to the office of a prophet, for the purposes of this book, we will simplify that conversation by saying a woman can be either. Philip's four daughters prophesied as did Mary and Elizabeth.[3] Anna was not alone as one who speaks for God.

In fact, key to the prophecy of Pentecost was that the "daughters shall prophesy" (Joel 2:28). However, it was not long after the first outpouring of the Spirit that women got edged out of this ministry gift. According to Origen, who wrote during the second century, women could only prophesy outside the congregation.[4]

EXAMINING THE PASSAGE

Regarding the dilemma in Corinth then, if a woman can prophesy, what kind of speaking is she not to do? Some solve this by saying I Corinthians 14:34–35 means a woman cannot teach or preach but she can sing or testify if her husband approves. Some would say a woman can speak and preach but cannot teach. Others say she can teach and preach but cannot pastor. All of these answers are flawed. We have failed to properly understand the meaning of Scripture as it was written and as the original readers understood it. These two verses are not about teaching, preaching, or pastoring. Since the pivotal word here is "speak," this passage raises the question, "Can a woman use her voice in church or not?"

In the preceding passage, Paul had been encouraging the believers to speak out a word of prophecy or to speak a message in tongues followed by someone speaking the interpretation of the message. Was he now asking half the congregation not to speak at all? That would not make sense. The only record of a person in Scripture that God did not allow to speak was a man whom He struck dumb because of his unbelief.[5]

Looking closely, we see I Corinthians 14:34–35 reads: "Let your women *keep silent* in the churches, for they are *not permitted to speak*; but they are to be submissive, as the law also says. And if they want to learn something, let them ask their own husbands at home; for it is *shameful for women to speak* in church" (emphasis mine). As the *Apostolic Study Bible* says, "This passage is notoriously difficult to interpret."[6] Yet, we know that it cannot mean women cannot have a speaking role in the assembly of believers. There are too many other passages that put women speakers in a positive light. Elizabeth, for example, spoke out about the Lord as His Spirit prompted her. If it was a shame for her to speak, why did the Lord have her words recorded in Scripture? He silenced her husband yet inspired her to speak out boldly.

> *Elizabeth spoke out as the Spirit prompted her.*

In the same book where we read this prohibition about women in ministry, we also find Paul praising the churches that they "keep the traditions just as I delivered them to you," which included the rightfulness of a "woman who prays or prophesies" (I Corinthians 11:2, 5). Paul praises them for speaking out in the congregation and then *apparently* silences them three chapters later.

Sensible students stay aware of the cultures which originally read the Scriptures. If, for example, I lived in a culture where no one had ever heard of sheep, I would have to study and learn what sheep were before I understood Jesus' parables about sheep and shepherds. If I did not know what leaven was or what significance a coin would have to a woman in first-century Judaism, I would have to do some research so that His stories could mean something to me today. In a culture and era thousands of years removed from the original setting, it takes some research to recapture the original application of the message. From there, we can see how the same principles still work.

A popular way of explaining this passage has been to say that the early church was segregated by gender. According to this legend, whenever a woman wanted to get clarity on something, she would holler to her husband and ask him what was going on. If this were the case, why would only women shout questions and not the men? Among Gentile couples, everything was new to both the husbands and the wives alike. Archeological evidence reveals that the Corinthian church met in houses, so this explanation is insufficient. The only division in Jewish synagogues might have been between Jews and Gentiles. The only substantial evidence of gender divisions in a synagogue comes about a thousand years after the time of Paul, during the Middle Ages.[7]

Even if there were a physical separation between the men and the women, why didn't Paul just tell them to remove it and sit together? That would be easier than taking away the voice from the female half of the church. If new female believers were overexcited and talking too much during church, it seems Paul would have observed and dealt with that while there on location.

No Bible verse indicates that men and women should not learn together. Since Jesus let the children come right to Him while He taught, would He then turn and segregate the husbands and wives? No. He invited whole families and even applauded a single woman in Bethany who joined in to hear His teaching at the front of the room. No partitions or great chasm appear to have been fixed in His ministry. Therefore, it is not probable that there was a divider in the churches which provoked this discussion, but we still must determine the cause for the strong statements of I Corinthians 14.

DETAILS IN I CORINTHIANS 14:34–35

Verse 34 says a woman must be silent, meaning voiceless.[8] Verse 35 follows by saying it is a shame for women to speak in church! Obviously this command is not about a woman teaching in the church, as some have claimed, because the whole context leading up to these two verses is about gifts of the Spirit. Starting in chapter 12, the apostle showed how every part of the body was necessary and no one should say we have no need of another. Preceding that statement, he itemized a list of nine gifts of the Spirit. If women cannot speak in the church, then here is how a woman would see the gift list if she must be silent:

~~Word of wisdom~~
~~Word of knowledge~~
Faith
Gifts of healings
Working of miracles
~~Prophecy~~
Discerning of spirits
~~Different kinds of tongues~~
~~Interpretation of tongues.~~[9]

This would be in direct opposition to the theme of I Corinthians 12 that we not exclude any member of the body. Preceding the list, verse 7 promises that "the manifestation of the Spirit is given to each one" and at the conclusion verse 11 confirms that "the same Spirit works all these things, distributing to each one individually as He wills."

Clearly, vocal silence is not the goal of Paul's statement here. In I Corinthians 14:6, we learn that a person profits the congregation by coming with a prophesy, teaching, or other edifying words. Then believers are told to bring a psalm, teaching, tongue, etc., for the purpose of building each other up (14:26). So, if verses 34–35 are to mean women cannot do these things, it would have made a lot more sense for Paul to say so before encouraging everyone to be involved.

None of this clears up the statement "ask her husband at home." What is she supposed to ask him and how does that fit within the context of prophecies? Surely she was not supposed to ask him about the prophecy after they got home instead of when it was given. Some have suggested that this was about the judging of prophecies, which Paul discusses just before this statement. However, it would not do any good for her to discuss whether the prophecy was valid only after they had returned home.

As we delve into this discussion, you may notice that some Bible translations split verse 33 so that "as in all the churches" applies to the part about making women silent. Here is how it should read, from the NKJV:

> For God is not the author of confusion but of peace, as in all the churches of the saints. [End of section dealing with prophecy.]
>
> Let your women keep silent in the churches, for they are not permitted to speak; but they are to be submissive, as the law also says.

Compare that to the rendering in the ESV:

> For God is not a God of confusion but of peace. [End of section dealing with prophecy.]
> As in all the churches of the saints, the women should keep silent in the churches. For they are not permitted to speak, but should be in submission, as the Law also says.

The latter rendering is not faithful to the text as the second segment of verse 33 concludes the part about judging prophecies. It does not make good logic or good grammar to tack that phrase onto verse 34, making it say, "as in all the churches, so in the churches." Is Paul saying, "Since this is what we do in all the churches, this is what we need to do in all the churches"? No. Furthermore, when Paul uses a phrase like "as in all the churches," it comes at the end of the discussion, not the beginning. All the churches did not follow the practice of silencing women. Now, let us look step by step at what the Scripture does say.

"Let your women keep silent in the churches"
When reading I Corinthians 14, you will notice the discussion concerns the local congregation in Corinth. Then, suddenly the topic changes to address women "in all the churches." This seems out of place compared to the surrounding context. What caused this radical change in the flow of order? The discussion returns to prophecy and tongues right after these two verses. They actually sound like they are coming from another speaker.[10]

In his unpublished notes on Corinthians, Kelsey Griffin suggests that Paul was quoting the people in Corinth in I Corinthians 14:34–35.[11] Paul wrote this letter of I Corinthians in response to the letter brought to him from Chloe's

Paul quoted the Corinthians and then refuted their error.

people (1:11). What was she trying to inform him about or get his advice about? Problems and troublemakers. In fact, he references the letter from Corinth often and appears to quote it a few times. Much of the second half of I Corinthians appears to be in response to that letter. Among these believers, Jewish ways of thinking were in conflict with those of the Greeks.

Examples of Paul quoting them and responding are found throughout this epistle. In chapter 7, he says, "Now concerning the things of which you wrote to me," and then he quotes their letter: "It is good for a man not to touch a woman."[12] He refutes that statement and shows that a married man and woman *should* be together (7:1–2). Paul also responds to the inappropriate actions at the communion meals, saying, "What! Do you not have houses to eat and drink in?" This sounds a lot like his response to the statement silencing women as he says in 14:36, "What? came the word of God out from you?"[13] We will look at this more in a few pages.

One concern with this interpretation is that Paul did not announce that he was quoting from their letter. However, none of the other quotes from their letter are introduced formally either. Unlike English Bibles, "punctuation and quotation marks were not used in the original Hebrew and Greek languages of the Bible."[14] Translators have had to make the decision to use such punctuation based on the context of each passage.[15] Therefore, to set something off in quotes, one must look at the surrounding context or be aware of the source of the statement at hand. When Paul quotes Scripture, for example, we know it is Scripture because we recognize those original writings.[16]

"For they are not permitted to speak; but they are to be submissive"

Watch how Paul handles a church matter earlier in the same book. In I Corinthians 6:12 and 6:13, the text begins a quote without introducing it:

"All things are lawful for me."
Paul refutes this by saying, "but all things are not helpful."

"All things are lawful for me."
    He responds, "But I will not be brought under the power of any."

"Foods for the stomach and the stomach for foods."
    The apostle responds "But God will destroy both it and them."

We know these were quotes because of how he challenged the thought afterward. The people in Corinth would have recognized their words being read back to them. He taught them that we are not free to do "all things" or to fulfill any fleshly urge.[17] The statements surrounding these words oppose such concepts, and the rest of the Bible also lets us know the right view when we encounter such apparently conflicting passages.

Now that we know it is possible that Paul could be quoting from their letter or at least from a popular idea among them, we should look closely at the two verses in question. Why would he repeat their words? Because he "wishes to make clear exactly which positions he is responding to. Paul traces letter for letter, word for word their position," in order to refute it.[18]

Who could Paul be quoting in verses 34–35? Probably Jewish members of the church who wanted to continue their culture's tradition of women being silent in their synagogues.[19] It says "they are not permitted to speak," but does not say who is not permitting them. If you start reading from Genesis all the way to these verses, you will not find one instance where God instructs a woman to be quiet because of her gender. However, such written rules exist outside the Bible in Jewish commentaries on their law. Since the Corinthian church started in a Jewish context, there were tensions between the Jewish and Gentile believers.[20] The quote in 14:34–35 may have been a popular rabbi's perspective.[21]

"As the law also says"

We know women were actively involved in the Christian congregations because Paul had arrested them before he was converted.[22] They must have been out*spoken* to merit arrest (it was the message of Jesus which incriminated them). After his conversion, Paul embraced those he once persecuted. Furthermore, it does not seem like Paul to claim the Law as a source for silencing women: "as the law also says." Earlier in this same letter, he taught that the New Covenant fulfilled the Old, not that it duplicated it.[23] Elsewhere, he explained that we are not under obligation to Moses' law.[24] So, it is not like Paul to use the law of Moses to promote a rule it does not even mention.

Jews used the word "law" very loosely (the Hebrew word for law simply means "instruction"). Many referred to popular traditions and rabbinic explanations as the Oral Law. Jesus condemned the legalistic Jews who added such rules to the Law.[25] Devout Jews called their oral law the *Mishnah*. The *Talmud* was the commentary on the *Mishnah*, which was written down in the century after Paul.[26] According to these orally preserved traditions, for example, a man could divorce his wife, but a wife could not divorce her husband.[27] These oral laws justified the treatment of women as personal property. Even the historian Josephus referred to the rabbinic commentaries of the *Mishnah* and *Talmud* as the law.[28]

In the Talmud, it was "forbidden by Jewish traditions for women to speak in the synagogue."[29] Rabbis twisted the tenth commandment to classify women with animals. Three of the *Mishnahs* give this prayer for the Jewish male to pray:

> "Praise be to God he has not created me a Gentile;
> praise be to God that he has not created me a woman;

praise be to God that he has not created me an ignorant man."[30]

While it might be shocking to some to think that people could be so prejudiced, our world (and even some churches) hold pockets of such attitudes. God didn't find the woman He created to be a blight on His handiwork. In fact, until she arrived in the man's life, God said of him, "This is not good." The serpent wanted to destroy the woman. Those who demean women must consider what spirit they are of.

"And if they want to learn something, let them ask their own husbands at home"

In first-century Jewish culture, men spoke in public, not women,[31] and men gave testimony or conducted business, not women.[32] For example, Ben Sira said, "Do not converse much with women, as this will ultimately lead you to unchastity."[33] If a man believed that, no wonder he would call for silence from the females. If this kind of thinking was what all the to-do was about, then no wonder Chloe, leader of a house church, wrote to Paul asking him to help set some things straight!

The passage says "if" they want to learn, they must do so at home.[34] That does not sound like Paul. Can you imagine a preacher today telling a new believer that understanding the faith is totally random and optional? If you want to understand baptism; if you want to learn about God; if prayer interests you. When did it become optional for a Christian to learn? When the Lord instructed apostles, prophets, evangelists, pastors, and teachers to train and equip His body, did He wish for them to develop only the male half of the church and make spiritual development optional for the lady folk? No, every believer must learn and grow up into a mature faith.

Jews, however, did not encourage women to learn, so it would be easy for a rabbi to say, "*If* the women want to learn, do so at home." Contemporary with first-century Christians was a Jewish rabbi named Eliezar who said, "Rather should the words of the Torah be burned than entrusted to a woman . . . Whoever teaches his daughter the Torah is like one who teaches her obscenity."[35]

"For it is shameful for women to speak in church"
While it might be challenging to accept the idea of verses 34–35 as Paul quoting his opponents, I find it more shocking to think of Paul saying "it is shameful for women to speak in church." He has already endorsed the women who pray and prophesy in church or manifest other gifts of the Spirit involving the spoken word. Clearly, he does not find the female voice a shameful thing. Those against women preachers attempt to explain this as meaning that a woman can prophesy or pray, but not teach or give orders. Such a theory appears to say a woman can be trusted to speak words which bypass her mind, such as prophecy, but she cannot speak words that filter through her own thoughts and reasoning, such as teaching demands. This logic is like saying the female brain is deficient.

Verse 35 does not say it is a shame for a woman to think. Nothing in the context refers to teaching, preaching, or leading a church. For one to say this passage forbids women from teaching in church, one would have to already have that opinion to see it here, because it does not arise naturally out of this passage. We have to let it say only what it says: "shameful for women to speak in church." Consider how strong such a statement is: "The twice-repeated use of the basic Greek verb for oral communication *to speak* extends the range of the prohibition to any form of articulate expression. It applies to all manner of speech such as prayer, prophecy, tongues, interpretation, evaluation, teaching, and even to the whisper of women who might be tempted to ask their husbands a question during congregational worship."[36] I do not believe Paul ever restricted women like this. Someone in

Corinth was saying that women were not necessary and were even a disgrace in the church.

Shameful is a strong word. Did the Jews and their law say talking women were a shame? Rabbi Johanan indicated that talking to a woman would send a man to hell.[37] The oral law also taught that it was a "shame for a woman to let her voice be heard among men,"[38] and that "a woman's voice is a sexual excitement."[39] The word shame[40] in verse 35 would capture such notions. If Jews believed women were so dangerous, it is no surprise they would demand that women be silent. Elsewhere, Paul used the word shame to indicate filthy deeds including the blurring of gender distinctions and works of darkness a believer should not even talk about.[41] If the situation was merely that wives were interrupting or being clumsy about learning, the word shame would be too strong in that context. Apparently the Jewish faction in Corinth was responsible for making these hostile accusations. If Paul did not buy into Jewish biases against women, why did he quote these words? So he could respond: "What? came the word of God out from you?" (14:36, KJV). He succinctly answers such notions, which response we examine in the next chapter.

> *Popular Jewish thinking viewed women as a moral threat and even considered them to be shameful.*

4 | *He Called Deborah: Women as Leaders*

Can women serve only when a man does not respond to the call?

> *Now Deborah, a prophetess, the wife of Lapidoth, was judging Israel at that time. And she would sit under the palm tree of Deborah between Ramah and Bethel in the mountains of Ephraim. And the children of Israel came up to her for judgment (Judges 4:4–5).*

News stories often waste time on celebrities: people who are famous for being famous. Real news gives the public information about things that change their lives: political concerns, financial matters, and threats to the populace. I find it laughable that news media spend time on the misfired romances of a pop singer or think the public needs to know when a movie star gets arrested for drunk driving.

Deborah was not a celebrity.

Celebrities become widely known because of their performance. We should celebrate people for what they are on the inside—character, integrity, vision. Too many social icons became idols just because of looks, family name, or simply because they had a good agent. In the kingdom of God, things should not work this way. We should not propel a person to center stage simply because she has a beautiful singing voice or he can "preach the house down." We need men and women of God who become something significant before they do something significant.

Deborah's character preceded her popularity. She did not have a throne or studio. People came to her for her wisdom, not because she had any special title. Her homespun wisdom under a palm tree brought Hebrew people searching her out. God's people would do well to learn from her today, too. Let your character precede your ministry work.

Gideon, on the other hand, became known because of what he did, not because of who he was. He was also a judge of Israel like Deborah, but his heroic actions outpaced his character development. After his time in the spotlight, he turned to idolatry. Samson's character also lagged behind his influence. His personal fame preceded the development of moral integrity.

In contrast to icons like Gideon and Samson, two other judges (or governors) of the early nation of Israel became well-known for their character before getting an official title and status. The integrity of both Samuel and Deborah prepared others to follow them when the time came. People did not come to them because of their looks, claims to fame, or military genius. They came to them because they were moral anchors.

The Deborahs of this day inspire us to serve God because they have lasting influence. Many believers go to such spiritual anchors for advice. They may not have college degrees, brass name-plates on their doors, or official titles, but they are there when you need them. They make you feel important. They have understanding even if they cannot give a quick answer. They are the people you want to be like when you grow up (even if you are sixty years old).

Deborah was not looking to make a name for herself. The people sought her out because she had the integrity they needed in a leader. As judge of Israel, she took charge of setting God's people free. As an invitational leader, she gave

Barak a chance to be a heroic army commander. He asked for her help and she told him what to do to win. God put the enemy commander in the hands of Jael, another woman, who finished what the men had been unable to do.

Unlike other judges, Deborah did not gain her reputation from her exploits. The people already knew she could be trusted for wisdom and called her in to lead in crisis. Many promising young ministers skyrocket into the spotlight because of exceptional preaching ability. Unfortunately, many have not developed character that can keep pace with such fame and overexposure. They might crash and burn, thinking everything hinges on them, not the true doctrine, the life of separation, or the sacrifice of the elders who have paved the way for them.

Most of the judges in the Book of Judges became recognized leaders and judges *after* they had defeated the oppressing enemy, whereas Deborah's ministry began *before* the military victory. She was already recognized by the people as a wise and authoritative figure, indicated by the fact that people went to her to have their disputes settled.[1] Deborah was like another Moses to whom people came for judgment. She and Barak sang a song of victory much like the celebration after the crossing of the Red Sea.

The Book of Judges illustrates more about what not to do as a leader than about what to do. Gideon became a violent man and worshiped idols, Samson had a lust problem, and Jephthah made a rash vow. Deborah, however, was exemplary in every way, standing out from so many other judges who were immoral and caused many of the country's problems. She led because God called her to serve Him, and the people could see the value of her guidance. Samuel was the only other judge of Israel who had as many positive comments about his ministry. Deborah was a prophet first, before she became the governor. God recorded nothing negative about Deborah, unlike the rest of the judges who were males.

Deborah also served as a teacher. When people came to her as leader of the country, her instructions guided their lives. Barak obeyed her. She prophesied, governed, and directed. A man could not carry a heavier burden of service to the people of God. In this, she was like Samuel to whom people also came for counsel and who also did not lead in battle.[2] Deborah and Samuel were the only two prophetic judges. How amazing that the Scriptures would speak so positively of a woman in this role in a male-dominated culture.

> Deborah was a governor of Israel who prophesied, instructed, and guided the people.

ARE WOMEN ONLY BACK-UP MINISTERS?

Deborah was willing to share her power—give it away, in fact. She exemplified a servant-leadership style which put her in a different league from Samson, Gideon, and Jephthah. Unfortunately, some have used the Deborah story to say a woman can only serve the Lord if a man does not respond. A teaching arose by a well-known preacher in the first quarter of the twentieth century which would influence Pentecostal groups significantly. This preacher said God only called women when a man would not respond. Some picked up this statement and quoted it as if it were Scripture. The next generation of Pentecostals saw a dramatic drop in the number of women serving in pastoral ministry or even licensed to preach.[3]

Does God only call women if men are not doing the job? While I do not believe this, consider that even "if one were to grant this premise, it would hardly provide an argument against women's ministry today, given the fact that perhaps over half the world's population has yet to hear the gospel of Jesus Christ in a culturally intelligible way and that most of Christ's church, and presumably many of its teachers, remain too asleep to rise to his call."[4]

Early in my ministry, I remember calling a mentor of mine to ask questions about some dilemmas I faced in growing a church. One day he was not available to take my call and his wife offered to help if she could. I love his wife and thought highly of her as a prayer warrior and church leader, but I had not considered asking for her insights on pastoral issues. Reluctantly, I told her the situation I was facing but did not go into all the details because I did not expect her to have much insight on things like this. She gave me wisdom from heaven in handling that situation. I was shocked. This little woman was a good cook, a great prayer warrior, and a pastor to pastors. She never handed me a business card boasting of her spiritual expertise. You never see her speak at the church growth meetings. She does not parade herself or her wisdom. She is a Deborah whom I have discovered many people know about and go to for judgment. God did not give her an anointing because her husband was not available for the phone that day. He had already called her to what she does.

> *Deborah did not lead because there was no man available but because of the hand of God on her life.*

Notice that Deborah did not govern Israel because no man would respond. The battle where Barak balked at carrying his load arose while she was already leader. Deborah was more than a pinch-hitter; she was a well-qualified leader of men and women during troublesome times.

PAUL'S RESPONSE TO I CORINTHIANS 14:34-35

Paul would not reject a Deborah. The previous chapter took a close look at the Corinthians Jews who claimed a woman had to be silent in the church. After quoting them, he responded to this outrageous claim much the way we might respond to a man who thinks women only have an auxiliary place in the Kingdom. If a man told me that a woman could only serve where a man wouldn't, I might respond, "What? You have a direct line to God more than a woman does?" Consider what Paul said.

"Or did the word of God come originally from you? Or was it you only that it reached?"

First Corinthians 14:36–40 appears to be a block of text where Paul responded to some Jewish Christians and then he concluded the discussion of spiritual gifts. In 11:22, Paul also responded with "What?" and a sarcastic response to their outrageous behavior during communion service. Unfortunately, few modern translations give as strong a statement of surprise as the KJV's "What?" in 14:36. Perhaps the newer translators have followed the Calvinistic trend toward limiting women in ministry. There is more to it as well, as some argue the original text does not reflect such an abrupt response.[5] No matter with what intensity one should read his response, we recognize Paul was opposing something. If verses 34–35 are not a quote from Corinth, it is hard to understand what he is railing against.

Paul asked, "Did the Word of God come from you?" Those who do not believe Paul was responding to a Jewish quote would say he was upset with women making a ruckus in the church. However, Paul did not say "you" to women but to males (or both).[6] So, "Paul is now talking to the men, . . . Verses 34–35 clearly concern the women. Why doesn't the chiding of verse 36 continue to concern them? Why does it now aim at the men?"[7] Most likely because Paul was responding to Jewish misogynists and speaks to defend the involvement of women in church.

"If anyone thinks himself to be a prophet or spiritual"

This controversy regarding silencing women may have stemmed from an event where women were prophesying excessively or giving messages in tongues without an interpretation. I can see some Jewish men thinking the best way of handling this would be to issue an edict to reinforce their cultural practice to "keep the women out." Instead, Paul teaches carefully that everyone needs to come ready to participate in the service but be careful to not give an uninterpreted message or to speak too many prophecies. The problem was in how the spiritual gifts were being handled, not the gender of those being used by the Spirit.

Are men somehow more spiritual? Are only men prophets? Just because a person is a spiritual giant does not mean he can bully anyone else around. "If anyone thinks himself to be a prophet or spiritual, let him acknowledge that the things which I write to you are the commandments of the Lord," says verse 37. They tried to pull out the trump card of the Law but Paul responded with the "commands of the Lord."

"let him acknowledge that the things which I write to you are the commandments of the Lord"

It would be awkward to think that Paul's "commands of the Lord" are for women to be silent. The commands he mentioned began in chapter 11 where he addressed how everyone should behave in church and that they should stop the nonsense. The high point of this dialogue from there until this point is chapter 13 where love is the abiding principle and the command of the Lord.[8] If certain men wanted to silence women, they need to know this is not love. They were to bear with one another and consider others better than themselves, not beneath themselves.

The problems among the Corinthian believers, mentioned from 11:2 to 14:40, could be resolved only by that love so brilliantly defined in the thirteenth chapter: "Love suffers long and is kind; love does not envy; love does not parade itself, is not puffed up; does not behave rudely, does not seek its own, is not provoked, thinks no evil; does not rejoice in iniquity, but rejoices in the truth; bears all things, believes all things, hopes all things, endures all things" (13:4–7). It should be no surprise that this command comes sandwiched between discussions about prophecies, tongues, and word of knowledge. Even today many who are "super spiritual" need to heed the command to show love to their brothers and their sisters.

"But if anyone is ignorant, let him be ignorant"
Imagine new believers start attending your church and hear that King David danced before the Lord. Being ignorant of what this expression means exactly, these new believers jump into the aisles and bust a few moves they learned at the club they used to visit on Fridays. One overreaction that would solve such outrageous behavior would be for a leader to say, "No more dancing during church worship." The other wrong option would be to put in a disco ball, hire a worldly band and let everyone rock until they dropped. However, those extremes are not the right choices. The new believers simply need to learn to worship God freely without drawing attention to their bodies. Paul is doing a similar thing here regarding out-of-control spiritual gifts: don't stop women from participating, just teach them spiritual protocol.

Paul did not get hung up on this issue, however, nor did he let the church members get stuck here either. He said in verse 38, "But if anyone is ignorant, let him be ignorant." There will always be those hung up with their preconceptions or traditions. The church must move on to be what God has called it to be, including both men and women as participants in spiritual things.

"Therefore, brethren, desire earnestly to prophesy, and do not forbid to speak with tongues."
This verse is another hint that someone was trying to silence someone else. Verse 39 lets the second shoe fall, so to speak: do not forbid anyone from speaking as God moves them. In fact, all should eagerly desire to speak God-inspired words. This statement balances out verse 31 which also says, "For you can all prophesy one by one, that all may learn and

all may be encouraged." Paul helped them get over the hurdles of those who were talking out of turn, talking too much, and being prevented from talking altogether.

This whole block from 11:2–14:40 has the discussion of women's roles in spiritual gifts as bookends. In 11:5, women are to pray and prophesy in the congregation. At the conclusion, again they should not be forbidden to speak with tongues or to prophesy. The core of the dialogue is love. It appears that some very unloving things were happening in this spiritually active church setting. By dealing with the divisive issues and the women who were being pushed to the fringes, Paul gets to the heart of the matter: love.

"Let all things be done decently and in order"
Looking through the passage at the Corinthian church scene, it appears that some women were probably learning to operate in the gifts and in their excitement began to give prophecies while another was prophesying. They gave messages in tongues followed by messages in tongues. The place was in chaos and something had to be done. Not sure what to do, former Jewish men resurrected the old gag order against women in the synagogue.

Chloe and others were upset. They realized something needed to be done, but telling women they could not speak in tongues or give prophecies went too far. They wrote Paul a clearinghouse sort of letter that covered all the crazy issues that had come up in the church since he left.

Paul responded by explaining how messages in tongues should be handled and how to give prophecies in an orderly manner: tongues need interpretation and prophecies should not be given more than two in a service or at the most three. Then, he addressed the solution brought up by the Jews who thought silencing the women would be the proper resolution of the dilemma. Immediately he followed their narrow view with a rebuke. It would be like Paul saying:

> Did God's Word only come through you guys? Was it only for you (and not women, too)? If you folks think you are spiritual, discern this: what I am writing to you about loving each other and making room for everyone's gifting in the church is the Lord's Command (not the sayings of a dead rabbi). If someone wants to be stupid about this, he's ignorant. Ultimately, all of you should desire to prophesy and no one should be silenced from speaking in tongues. Just see that you do everything in a decent and orderly manner.[9]

Before ever addressing this issue of silencing women, verse 33 says, "God is not the author of confusion but of peace, as in all the churches of the saints." Later, verse 40 says, "Let all things be done decently and in order."

It was not gender roles that had to be defined, but the chaos in leadership and imbalanced interaction in the congregation. "The irony of all this is that the very scripture which has for centuries been interpreted as silencing female participation in the worship of the churches, may now be understood as declaring their equality."[10] Brothers, we should not get into conflict against our sisters over this passage which was written to stop such clashes in the first place.

SAVED BY YOUR CALLING

Women today need not only look to Deborah as a role model, but they also should do like Jael. When the enemy war captain ran and hid in her tent, she did not try to fight him like a man but took him down with tent peg and hammer.[11] She saw an opportunity to do something for God and His people. She knew she could not do battle like a man, so she did battle as a woman.

Our world is not hurting for more suits and ties but for more God-called workers. Women today need to step in where they can do the most for God. Deborah did not ask for the title of governor; her character caused people to ask for her wisdom and let her lead. A Hebrew judge was one who could make laws, govern, settle disputes, or punish someone.[12] She did not push her way into leadership, but stepped in because of the need. God is calling the unlikely ones and the ones others have overlooked to be part of His work. The true spirit of Pentecost must continue as it began, with female leaders.

Consider what Paul commanded Timothy regarding his ministry. He said, "Do not neglect the gift that is in you" (I Timothy 4:14). Unfortunately, many women have been told to neglect their gift. With Paul, I say, "Don't let it die!" You should reflect "on these things; give yourself entirely to them, that your progress may be evident to all" (4:15). Let your ministry enlarge you. Don't just talk about it and put it on business cards. If the Lord has called you to win souls, then do it! Apply yourself to the call of God on your life by study, prayer, and practice. Then, "in doing this you will *save* both *yourself* and those who hear you" (4:16).

> *A believer must give his or herself to his or her calling and ministry.*

Mae Iry found that by giving herself for the cause of God's kingdom, He would guide her each step of the way:

> Evidence of the divine hand on her life moved Bishop G. T. Haywood and the elders to ordain her at a conference in Indianapolis.
>
> Childhood polio left Mae with the right half of her face paralyzed. She spoke and ate with the mobile left half of her mouth and charmed everyone with an infectious one-sided grin. She forgot the lonely years of struggle and toil when the time came for her dream to become reality. In preparation to go she visited churches sharing her burden for China . . .
>
> Many days of tedious labor were necessary before they could renovate and occupy the run-down group of buildings that became their mission compound. Language study remained a major concern, but with Stiegie

(as her friends called her) services began immediately.
. . . Mae almost despaired of ever learning [Chinese]. Then a strange thing happened, though at first she couldn't make herself understood between services, when she began to preach the Holy Ghost touched that twisted mouth and she gave the Word with anointing and remarkable fluency. Those who knew her on both sides of the world remember an exuberant expression she often gave while preaching, in English or in Chinese; "Joy! Joy! Joy!"
During the language struggle time, Mae walked into the "downside kitchen" where the Chinese cooked their food. An old lady threw herself into Mae's arms weeping in urgent prayer. Suddenly, she broke into English as she received the Holy Ghost, praising God in a language unknown to her, but well-known to the missionary. The Lord spoke to Mae explicitly through the old lady and gave her promises that she would stand on as long as she lived.[13]

The soul you save by your ministry might be your own.

You have a job to do. Souls will die without the Lord if you excuse yourself from evangelism. You must do what the Lord has called you to and apply yourself to it. A fireman who never trains may die due to his own negligence. Give yourself to the call as if your life depended on it. By doing this, you will save yourself and those who hear you. How important is it that a woman be able to fulfill her ministry? Her salvation might depend on it. Sisters, apply yourself to your calling so that you might save yourself and those who hear you!

5 | *He Called Priscilla: Women as Teachers*

Can a woman teach Bible truths?

> *Greet Priscilla and Aquila, my fellow workers in Christ Jesus, who risked their own necks for my life, to whom not only I give thanks, but also all the churches of the Gentiles (Romans 16:3–4).*

Some have argued that a woman can prophesy but not teach. This argument comes mainly from Calvinists who may have never experienced what it means to prophesy. The Calvinist camp would argue that a woman can prophesy but that she cannot teach. One of the claims of Calvinist theology is that God has ceased to work in the gifts of the Spirit. So, essentially, this influential movement is convincing millions that women no longer have a speaking role in the church. Pentecostals, however, experience prophecies today as did the early believers.

Prophecy is a word given by God through a believer. Many Pentecostals would suggest that it takes more spiritual authority, more of a walk with God, and prayerful dedication to give a word of prophecy than to teach Scripture. Through prophecy God convicts hearts of unbelievers, even causing them to fall down before Him and turn from a life of sin (I Corinthians 14:24–25). While this often comes as an isolated event when a person speaks for the Lord during a church worship service, it regularly occurs during preaching when the speaker says God-given words that convict the hearts of those listening.

Teaching, on the other hand, informs and educates believers. While this is a spiritual work, it can be a simple presentation from God's Word. During my dad's conversion, even before he had received the Spirit, he taught others what he was learning about the Bible and the gift of the Holy Ghost. How much more effective could a Spirit-filled woman be at teaching a Bible lesson?

> *Teaching, like prophesy, informs and instructs the hearers of spiritual things.*

In the church, those being taught are already in the faith and should be able to discern if they are being taught incorrectly. Therefore, if a woman can do the more spiritually advanced task of prophesying, she certainly should be able to do the work of teaching those who already know the truth, or at least most of it.

Before Oma Ellis knew she would be a minister, it was the working of spiritual gifts that convinced her to teach and preach for the Lord:

> One day after I had spoken in tongues at length, I opened my Bible and a verse of Scripture just leaped out at me: "Wherefore let him that speaketh in an unknown tongue pray that he may interpret" (I Corinthians 14:13). So I asked the Lord to give me the interpretation. . . .
>
> As I prayed in tongues again, the interpretation came: "I have called you to preach My Word."
>
> I was astonished. Like my father, I did not believe that God called women to preach. Even though Bertha Clinton pastored the Sherman church where I received the Holy Ghost, I still did not accept the idea very well. The evangelist, Brother Stallones, had done the preaching, and I could accept that. I did not want to be a woman preacher.

I got right up from praying and felt like I did not want to pray any more. Things were getting out of hand. "Maybe the devil had gotten a hold of me and I hadn't gotten a true interpretation," I thought.

I did not pray any more that day. But the next morning I felt an urgency to pray. Again the message in tongues came, "I have called you to teach."

"Well," I thought, "I can go along with the idea of being a teacher." So I pushed the whole thing to the back of my mind and felt more relaxed about it.

The next day in prayer the call came again in tongues and interpretation, "I have called you to preach and to teach My Word."

The turmoil returned, so I sat right down and wrote a letter to Winnie. "It's getting so that I'm afraid to get on my knees to pray. I keep hearing 'I have called you to preach' over and over. Do you suppose the devil is talking to me?"

Winnie wrote right back. "Brother Stallones, Sister Clinton, and others here in Sherman have received a witness that God would call you sometime into the ministry. Oma, just keep on praying and studying the Word. God will work it all out in His time."[1]

IN CORINTH, EPHESUS, AND ROME

Priscilla served the Master as a vessel of honor and we see a few honorable mentions about her in Scripture. She and her husband had come from Rome, and ran a business in Corinth where they met Paul. Paul worked in the same trade with them. Soon, Priscilla and her husband Aquila became great assets for the work of the Lord. Being that they had a good income, they probably had a large enough home to host a church.

After spending some time in Corinth, Paul moved on, taking Priscilla and Aquila with him to Ephesus. After Paul left them there, a great preacher named Apollos arrived. Priscilla and Aquila took him in and explained the truth more thoroughly to him. Apollos then powerfully convinced many Jews with the full message about Jesus. Priscilla and Aquila's student was so well-schooled in the faith that Paul later referred to him as his own peer when he wrote to the Corinthians.

Paul honored Priscilla, also called Prisca. For Scripture to mention the house belonging to both Aquila and Priscilla shows that she was on the same level with him since the man was typically owner of the house in that day.[2] In Corinth, it appears Aquila was the better known of the two, possibly because of his business success. There, his name precedes his wife's name indicating that he was the more recognized individual.[3] In Ephesus and Rome, Priscilla's name precedes her husband's, indicating that she was the more prominent leader there.[4] Given that this couple had house churches in Rome and previously in Ephesus, for Priscilla to be a leader, she must have been a speaking, teaching leader in that setting, not just a hostess serving punch.[5]

Paul applauded this couple and spoke highly of them. The description of how she and he taught Apollos matches the same verbiage used to describe Paul as a teacher.[6] In fact, the passages of Scripture that many have used to say women should not teach or lead were written in letters that went to the churches where Priscilla was a leader! One commentator asks, "Writing to the Corinthian church, where Priscilla housed and fed him for eighteen months, is [Paul] insulting her by telling her to be silent in the church?"[7] Of course this was not Paul's intention, as revealed in the previous chapters regarding I Corinthians 14:34–35.

Priscilla was a church leader like any other. If Paul had a problem with what she was doing, he certainly had an odd way of saying so. He never hedged what he had to say to someone. He called people out in his letters, naming names and making a scene about their wrong doing. If Priscilla was wrong to be teaching and leading ("having authority") then he would have certainly said so. Instead, he consistently commended her. Writing to another city where Priscilla did not minister or teach, Paul said that a woman leader must be a teacher (Titus 2:3). How much emphasis do our modern churches put on women being "teachers of good"?

Some have rejected the idea of women teachers because of a perplexing passage also written by Paul. In debates and conversations regarding women in leadership, I Timothy 2:11–12 in particular always becomes the focus of attention:

> Let a woman learn in silence with all submission. And I do not permit a woman to teach or to have authority over a man, but to be in silence.

Those who read this passage should be careful not to overlook the historical and cultural situation which Timothy faced at the time Paul wrote this to him.

BACKGROUND BEHIND I TIMOTHY 2:11–12

Paul wrote to urge Timothy who was stationed in Ephesus to "charge some that they teach no other doctrine," because false teaching was at work in the church (I Timothy 1:3). This included "fables and endless genealogies, which cause disputes" and not just among the women (1:4). He also warned the younger church leader that "some, having strayed, have turned aside to idle talk, desiring to be teachers of the law," but unfortunately they were "understanding neither what they say nor the things which they affirm" (1:6–7). Too much confusion and wrong teaching had created a chaotic mess which Paul wished he could come straighten out himself (3:15; 4:3). He warned against the "old wives' fables" (4:7) and women who had already turned toward Satan (5:15).

About 35 percent of the letter deals with correcting false teaching.[8] While the false teachers included two men named Hymenaeus and Alexander, even some women were saying things "they ought not" (5:13). The remedy was for Timothy to teach and speak out clearly (4:11, 13) and to be sure those who were teaching the truth received proper support and not mistreatment (5:18–20). He had no tolerance for those who would teach something that was not of Christ (6:3–5). After addressing measures to set the church in order, Paul concluded by reemphasizing this, saying, "O Timothy! Guard what was committed to your trust, avoiding the profane and idle babblings and contradictions of what is falsely called knowledge—by professing it some have strayed concerning the faith" (6:20–21).[9]

Paul told his understudy to instruct certain believers to teach the truth.[10] If Paul had believed that only men could teach, he would have said "appoint faithful males to teach," but he did not say it this way. All Scriptures referring to a teaching ministry are gender-inclusive, allowing both men and women to respond to the Lord's call to teach.

All Scriptures referring to a teaching ministry are gender-inclusive, allowing both men and women to respond to the Lord's call to teach.

DETAILS WITHIN I TIMOTHY 2:11–12

Paul said, "Let a woman learn in silence with all submission. And I do not permit a woman to teach or to have authority over a man, but to be in silence." We can examine this passage piece by piece. Zooming in on the text might help us get the true meaning in focus.

"Let a woman learn"

In Jewish culture, many women were barred from learning the Scriptures. One Rabbi said, "Rather should the words of the Torah be burned than entrusted to a woman . . . Whoever teaches his daughter the Torah is like one who teaches her obscenity."[11] They did not let women learn since the purpose of education was so one could teach others.[12]

Yet Paul said a woman should learn. Jesus also encouraged women to learn about Him and applauded those who chose to. Education equips. When we teach women in our churches and Bible schools, we are preparing them for leadership.[13]

"in silence"

Some readers of I Corinthians 14:34 think this passage is a parallel to that one. However, it does not use the same Greek word for "silence." In the Corinthian quote we examined previously, the Greek word translated as silence refers predominantly to not speaking a word.[14] In I Timothy, the apostle used a different Greek word which does not refer to voicelessness but quietness.[15] In another epistle, Paul told some busybodies who were not working at all to "work in quietness," using this same word.[16]

The use of this word in both passages appears to apply to the domestic sphere, another reason they should be translated similarly.[17] Furthermore, the word for such calmness mirrors the word used for the "peaceable" life in I Timothy 2:2.[18] No one should take this passage to say women cannot speak in the assembly, especially since it says nothing about a church service. If it meant absolute silence, then it would require the woman to be silent everywhere.

"with all submission."

This cannot mean that a woman must be in submission to all men. The Word of God does not call women to submit to men. A woman need only submit to her man, her husband. The full sense of this passage will make better sense through that lens, as the next chapter will explore.

"And I do not permit"

Some have argued that this phrase means it was just a temporary thing. Was there some local issue going on where Paul said, "I am not letting the women be involved in ministry right now"? Or does this reflect his personal bias against women in ministry whereas other leaders might allow them? We cannot make much of a Bible passage with guess work.

We could say, however, that if the phrase "I permit not a woman" applies to all women everywhere, then it is certainly a broad statement. Such an idea uproots the precedents set by Deborah, Huldah, Miriam, Esther, Mary, Junia, and many others. One scholar says, "It would be surprising if an issue that would exclude at least half the body of Christ from a ministry of teaching would be addressed in only one text."[19] Paul says this strongly and makes it obvious that this is not just a passing issue. The answer to the riddle of these two verses lies elsewhere.

"a woman"

Some have offered that the dilemma was "a woman" and not all women who were to be restricted from teaching and leading. Perhaps, they say, there was a divisive woman making things hard for others in Ephesus. If that were the case, however, would Paul not have confronted her while he was there or simply have named the woman to avoid ambiguity? Paul certainly would not have wanted to prevent Priscilla from being instrumental in reaching another Apollos.

"to teach or"

Some say this passage means a woman cannot teach in the church, although nothing has been said in or around the passage about church work. Those who believe this, though, might claim a woman can give private counsel in her home, using Priscilla as an example.

The thought that a woman could only teach and minister in her home or other private setting reveals ignorance of the first-century church setting. We find no separate set of rules for ministry in a home versus ministry in a public building. The earliest churches were in people's homes. If a woman can only minister at home, Priscilla could have preached the house down since church was in her house. A woman's ministry is not limited to the kind of building she might be in. The church is us—not a building or location. God placed women as well as men as members in His body to minister to His body and to the lost.

"to have authority"

While the focus of our chapter is on a woman teaching, this verse often gets hijacked at the sight of the word authority. Some say a woman cannot have any leadership role, forgetting about Deborah and other great female leaders God has sent along. We will look more in depth at this topic in Esther's chapter.

I used to believe that this passage meant a woman can only do ministry if she is submitted to a man or a pastor.[20] However, that is not what the verse says. It does not say, "She can teach as long as she is submitted." The ASV translates verse 12 as "But I permit not a woman to teach, nor to have dominion over a man." For that matter, nowhere do the Scriptures teach anyone to take dominion over another human being. More on this later.

"over a man,"

In the line of thinking that this passage is only about a woman then the contrasting person in question, a man, might need to be identified as well. Was there only one man whom this one woman was not to teach? Of course not.

For obvious reasons, some take I Timothy 2:11–12 to mean a woman cannot teach men.[21] How then do we reconcile that concept with the instances of women teaching men we find in Scripture? Priscilla was a woman who taught a man, and Paul only had good to say about her.[22]

"but to be in silence"
This cannot mean a woman is to be seen and not heard. This does not mean voicelessness, but calmness. There was some kind of uproar in Ephesus that needed help.

In another place, Paul wrote the words of a verse which commands men and women: "Let the word of Christ dwell in you richly in all wisdom, teaching and admonishing one another in psalms and hymns and spiritual songs, singing with grace in your hearts to the Lord" (Colossians 3:16). Priscilla, as co-leader of the church in her home, would have taught, admonished, and helped others grow in wisdom. Every godly woman should do this to one extent or another, depending on how much "ministry reach" the Lord gives them.

I think of the powerful women who have influenced my life by their speaking, writing, and godly living. Nona Freeman powerfully influenced a generation to give themselves to the service of the Lord. What if she were only allowed to speak to women or only to two or three males at a time? I thank God she understood His Word well enough to keep on preaching and ministering in the absence of and even after the death of her husband. We have many elect ladies in our churches that can powerfully defend the truth.

EXEMPLARY FEMALE LEADERS

The glimpses we see of Priscilla in the Bible show that this woman who is often mentioned before her husband as being a person of great importance to believers in many places.[23] I suppose one could contend that women like Junia, Anna, and Priscilla could be leaders in churches because they were married.[24] However, Paul indicated that an unmarried woman has more of a chance to serve the Lord since she is not distracted with pleasing her husband.[25] For each outstanding woman we glimpse in Scripture, there were scores more serving the Lord throughout the Roman Empire. Fortunately, Priscilla is not alone in the prestigious role of leading a church in her home.

Women who had churches in their homes include Nympha, Mary the mother of John Mark, Chloe, Lydia, and others.[26] Homes in that day could have hosted as many as seventy people. The gospel was exploding and multiple house churches sprang up in the same cities. I would love to see the church explode so much that we too would not see women as emergency overflow leaders but as authentic, God-called leaders in the harvest.

Wesley became convinced when he saw God doing a sovereign work through his mother and later through Mary Fletcher. Men today stand to be persuaded that women are called by God when they see Him at work through them. Daughter works and new church plants are waiting to begin if only a woman will heed the call. The fields are ready for harvest, we have prayed for laborers, and we must now accept those the Master has called to work in the field.

> *The fields are ready for harvest, we have prayed for laborers, and we must now accept those the Master has called to work in the field.*

NOT JUST TEACHERS, BUT LEADERS

Paul wrote his first letter to Timothy in Ephesus to stop false teaching (1:19–20; 5:19–20; 6:20–21). Priscilla may have been there when he wrote this. If she was not there when the first letter came, she was when the second one arrived. Perhaps Paul sent her and her husband back there from Rome to help stabilize things.[27] The words he used invite both male and female teachers and workers in the church.[28]

To lead a flock of believers, one must teach. You cannot make disciples without teaching. You cannot grow a church without teaching. Every believer can contribute in the church with words: either prophecy, a song, or teaching.²⁹ If a man or woman has learned the teachings of the Kingdom, they should be soon ready to share them with others (Hebrews 5:12).

Remember the sequence in I Corinthians 12:28 that God has called these in the church:

> First apostles,
> second prophets,
> third teachers

Junia and others have shown us that a woman can be an apostle. Anna, Hulda, Elizabeth, Philip's four daughters, and others prove that women can prophesy and be prophets. Now, Priscilla and others show us that a woman can be a teacher. Comparing the use of various Greek words on teaching reveals that the teaching women did was parallel to the teaching men did.³⁰ These ministry gifts are for whomever the Lord our God shall call.

In thousands of places around the world, women have brought the gospel and souls went from darkness to His marvelous light. Nothing in Scripture forbids these women missionaries from also teaching, training, and discipling those new souls in the Kingdom. Paul, the church planter, referred to several as coworkers; in other words, they were on the level of the apostle.

Even when referring to women who teamed up with him, Paul called them fellow laborers just as he did the men.³¹ This word simply meant "a person who shared the same trade" therefore referring to one who worked in the same manner as the apostle.³² Paul's fellow laborers would oversee congregations, evangelize and instruct, and do a variety of other ministry activities.³³ Paul mentioned two female fellow laborers, Euodia and Syntyche, who had "fought at his side"³⁴ for the sake of the gospel. It appears the people in Philippi, the place where we meet Lydia, were quite open to women in leadership.[35]

Priscilla risked her own neck for Paul.[36] Junia suffered imprisonment for the Gospel.[37] Mary, Tryphena, and Tryphosa labored much in the Lord: they were hard workers![38] Even if a woman cannot play professional football or be in heavy infantry, she can be in the harvest field and on the front lines for God!

In the sixteenth chapter of Romans, Paul mentions more men than women, yet, of those, he mentions seven women in ministry, which exceeds the number of ministering men whom he praises. Chrysostom said, "The women of those days were more spirited than lions, sharing with the Apostles their labors for the Gospel's sake. In this way they went traveling with them and also performed all other ministries."[39] Clearly, women were not restricted from ministry roles. Paul did not say they just worked with him but that they worked. More than just apostle-helpers, some women were apostles in their own right.

Paul understood the Lord to call women to serve Him, not just to tag along with the men. Some have said the New Testament mentions more men in ministry than women. To them, this is "evidence" that there should be far more men in ministry than women. However, if we consider the mentions of women in demanding situations, maybe we would conclude that more women should be in ministry than men (Romans 16:1-12, Philippians 4:3). If we followed the numbers in Romans 16, we would say two-thirds of the ministers in any given church should be women.[40] I would not argue for any quota, however. We should encourage as many men and as many women to minister as the Lord will call.

Paul expected the believers to submit to women such as Priscilla. His fellow laborers were not just cheerleaders. Speaking of fellow laborers, he told the believers "submit to such, and to everyone who works and labors with us."[41] This would mean the male and female fellow laborers were to be followed and obeyed as the saints would Paul. Suddenly we see women were more than just teachers but confirmed leaders in the church. Paul was not technically pushing an agenda of women in ministry any more pointedly than he pushed for men in ministry. Paul simply had an agenda to spread the gospel. Paul spoke of men in ministry and women in ministry in a blended discussion as if it was totally natural, not some oddity.[42] A church in revival will naturally produce women in ministry.

With all of this in view, then, why did Paul write such words in I Timothy 2:11–12? The next chapter will address this in depth.

6 | *He Called Sarah: Women as Daughters*

Does I Timothy 2:11–12 prohibit women from teaching men?

> *Wives, likewise, be submissive to your own husbands, that even if some do not obey the word, they, without a word, may be won by the conduct of their wives, when they observe your chaste conduct accompanied by fear. Do not let your adornment be merely outward—arranging the hair, wearing gold, or putting on fine apparel—rather let it be the hidden person of the heart, with the incorruptible beauty of a gentle and quiet spirit, which is very precious in the sight of God. For in this manner, in former times, the holy women who trusted in God also adorned themselves, being submissive to their own husbands, as Sarah obeyed Abraham, calling him lord, whose daughters you are if you do good and are not afraid with any terror (I Peter 3:1–6).*

Sarah was a modest woman who did not rely on glitz and glam to make herself attractive. Historically, Pentecostal and Holiness movements have emphasized separation from the world in how we look.[1] Sarah exemplified such things but had no daughters to pass her character on to. Just as we can all claim father Abraham as being our role model for faith,

Just as those of faith are children of Abraham, so godly women are daughters of Sarah.

women in the church today become the daughters Sarah never had. This chapter is not just about modesty, but also about whether it is immodest for a woman to teach a man.

Just as the Lord called Abraham and Sarah to serve Him by going to the Promised Land and having a promised son, Pentecostal women ministers are those who have responded to the call of God in their lives. Kenter Doje tells how she came to teach her people in India about Him:

> As boundless happiness in the Lord filled me, I started feeling very strongly for the people of my birth in Arunachal Pradesh. I kept thinking that as I am a mere youth, no one would listen to my speaking. This thought pained my heart, so I begged the Lord in prayer to grant my return to Arunachal. . . . God gave me a burden. That means I'm called. When I had a great burden, that meant God wanted me to go. . . .Since I had almost forgotten my mother tongue, Adi, I behaved almost like a beginner for some time, but I prayed to God saying, "Lord, you have sent me back to preach your Gospel to my people, but what can I tell them if I do not speak the dialect properly?" Not very long after, I was able to speak, converse and explain the Word of God to them. I had thought that my friends might think me a pretender at not knowing my mother tongue, but now as I started teaching them the Word of the Lord, the people were very eager to listen. This made me very happy.[2]

God did not only call this woman to serve Him, He revived her ability to speak the language so she could teach!

Of course, anecdotal references are not enough to convince those opposed to women in ministry. Let us again visit a battleground passage:

> Let a woman learn in silence with all submission. And I do not permit a woman to teach or to have authority over a man, but to be in silence.

While this chapter is about the words regarding women in I Timothy 2:11–12, I have included the words from I Peter 3 as well, because the two passages obviously parallel one another. This fact and the internal clues in I Timothy 2 let us know that this is a message primarily to married couples.

CONTEXT OF THE PASSAGE

This statement about a woman learning "in silence" comes in a chapter that begins with Paul exhorting that prayer be made for everyone including civil leaders (2:1–2). He explained that such prayers were in keeping with God's own nature because He wanted all to come to the truth (2:3–4). The key truth Paul presented was about the one God and one mediator, Jesus Christ (2:5–7). Then he addressed topics covering personal character. For men, this meant they would be those who prayed with pure hearts, without "wrath and doubting" (2:8).

The men apparently were riled about something, causing Paul to urge them to pray "without wrath and doubting." This could easily be translated as they were manifesting "anger" and "disputing."[3] With a false teaching forbidding marriage relations, as referenced in I Timothy 4:3, one may not be surprised to know husbands were full of wrath and disputing, possibly toward the false teachers. The heresy at work within the congregation was probably powered by a spirit of contention, stirring up anger among the brothers. God's men could not be holy and be arguing at the same time. Consistently, we find a need for peace and quietness in an Ephesian church facing false doctrine and church conflict.

The aged church-planter wrote under the power of the Spirit for women to "adorn themselves in modest apparel, with propriety and moderation, not with braided hair or gold or pearls or costly clothing, but, which is proper for women professing godliness, with good works" (2:9–10). The Ephesian women needed to be reminded of these things. Many women in that culture used jewelry to attract attention to themselves either in goddess worship, as prostitutes, or to flaunt their wealth. A godly woman, especially one who wanted to respond to the call of God, would only harm her testimony by letting extravagant accessories distract from the message.

Western society edges women into non-realistic molds as well. Actress Jennifer Aniston said,

> The media create this wonderful illusion, but the amount of airbrushing that goes into those beauty magazines, the hours of hair and makeup. It's impossible to live up to because it's not real.[4]

Celebrity Cindy Crawford shared similar sentiments:

> I think women see me on the cover of magazines and think that I never have a pimple or bags under my eyes. You have to realize that's after two hours of hair and makeup, plus retouching. Even I don't wake up looking like Cindy Crawford.[5]

It appears that the issue of forcing women into an impossible role is an age old problem.

This passage discussing ornate hairdos[6] parallels similar principles in I Peter 3:3–6 when speaking to married women:

> Do not let your adornment be merely outward— arranging the hair, wearing gold, or putting on fine apparel—rather let it be the hidden person of the heart, with the incorruptible beauty of a gentle and quiet spirit, which is very precious in the sight of God. For in this manner, in former times, the holy women who trusted in God also adorned themselves, being submissive to their own husbands, as Sarah obeyed Abraham, calling him lord, whose daughters you are if you do good and are not afraid with any terror.

Sarah exemplified a respectful wife; her attitude illustrated true beauty. Kings coveted this beautiful woman. The Lord protected her and answered her prayer for a child even in her old age.

Gaudiness is a form of insubordination. In that first-century culture, women wore gold and jewels in their artfully braided hairstyles. When their accessories "were of precious materials, fringed with gold, held firm by pins or little gold buckles embroidered with pearls or other precious stones, they lost all utilitarian character, and passed into the category of jewels."[7] Tertullian, an early Christian writer, complained about the "wasted pains on arranging your hair—what contribution can this make to your salvation? . . . You perpetrate unbelievable extravagances to make a kind of tapestry of your hair."[8]

The wearing of earrings is not a new thing either. "Seneca said scathingly that some women wore on a single ear the value of two or three estates. Ear-rings were often very heavy and, through wearing them, women sometimes badly distorted the shape of their ears."[9] One woman boasted of her wealth, which she wore in her ears. Her husband found her behavior infuriating, saying he was glad he did not have a daughter for he would have to cut her ears off "to put a stop to such nonsense."[10] Hyperbole notwithstanding, the Apostolic movement has traditionally upheld the biblical teachings against extravagance in adornment and so elevated the role of the woman to be whom God created her rather than her being molded by the world's image.[11]

Rebecca Johnson is one such daughter of Sarah with a gentle and humble spirit. While attending graduate school with her, her testimony and godly example moved me. She tells how liberating she found principles of modesty to be:

> Let me share with you how the weight of my soul was lifted. My biggest role-models in middle school were the Spice Girls; I covered my room with their

posters. It wasn't until it was "too late" did I learn that my examples were leading me down a path of a distorted understanding of the image of God. God's image is purposeful, but I could not grasp that purpose because of the examples I was following. I was allowing Hollywood to teach me womanhood. God designed and gave purpose to woman, but here I was letting the Spice Girls and any other pop-star sell me a cheap, unauthentic replica of beauty.

I boasted in this new false-identity as "this is who I am, like it or not." As prideful, arrogant, and confident as I was, sadly, I was blind. What I toted as self-expression and freedom was really bondage and spiritual slavery. I felt empty. I never felt good enough to keep up with the image of Hollywood, yet I would say I was free. I needed the image of God restored in my life because the image of Hollywood was exhausting, tiring and unattainable. I wanted to be a woman, but I couldn't seem to exactly find out how.

They flood the magazines, the commercials, and the movies with images that are not even real, they're edited, manipulated and cropped to create a false identity, but I was about to encounter the real. I was 22-years-old when I was exposed to the real image of beauty, which is the Lord himself. It is a presence that I long and yearn for every day. I do not follow the examples of Hollywood for an image anymore but I now pursue the freedom that comes from the holiness of God--the opportunity to celebrate the beauty of womanhood.[12]

> *"I do not follow the examples of Hollywood for an image anymore but I now pursue the freedom that comes from the holiness of God— the opportunity to celebrate the beauty of womanhood."*
> *— Rebecca Johnson*

More young women need godly role models in the church and in the pulpit to set an example of what godly womanhood is like. Young men also benefit from godly women leaders because this sets ideals before them that they should look for in a future spouse.

Peter taught wives to have modest speech toward their husbands and modest appearance to the world. Specifically, he addressed wives with unsaved husbands. Paul approached the same subjects, only addressing adornment first and how they treated a husband second. A man's wife makes him look good. She is his jewelry, so to speak. Her jewelry is her sweet spirit.[13] Women attracting lustful attention from other men would not make for a quiet home or a peaceful husband.

> *Paul, like Peter, encouraged modest behavior among wives who might upend the harmony of the home.*

The context of I Timothy 2 begins with reference to public life and a statement to men regarding their behavior "everywhere," not just in a church setting. "In like manner also," the command to the wives should not be considered a church-only thing. This is a universal ruling for women to be modest. It appears also as a universal call for women to behave properly toward their husbands and not try to preach at them or control them, as has been understood by many students of Scripture for generations.[14] Therefore, we should not quickly assume that verses 11–12 refer to women teaching or having authority in the church.

WINNING AN UNSAVED HUSBAND

This passage from I Timothy likely refers to women reaching misguided or unsaved husbands just as I Peter 3:1–6 does. For example, a godly man would not have to be taught to lift up sinless hands "without wrath and doubting" as I Timothy 2:8 commands. Paul's intentions seem similar to Peter's: to ask the new female believers to back off, so to speak. Peter instructed wives concerning their husbands that "if some do not obey the word, they, without a word, may be won by the conduct of their wives, when they observe your chaste conduct accompanied by fear" (I Peter 3:1–2).

Timothy had to deal with something similar, but Paul spoke to it in stronger terms. Paul and Peter both told the women to throttle back their words and learn quietness. Artemis worship threatened masculinity in Ephesus where Timothy was working when Paul wrote this letter.[15] The female-centered religion of Artemis (a.k.a., "Diana") put women in the lead, at least in their own minds. If wives had been converted before their husbands, they might wish to teach them and dominate the Christian religion, as well. Notice the distinction between how the *women* are to present themselves publicly in I Timothy 2:9–10 and how *a woman* is to behave in verses 11–12. The passage speaks especially to the relationship between a wife and her husband. With this passage in context and in comparison to I Peter 3:1–6, it makes perfect sense that a wife should submit and not try to teach or take authority over her husband.

One might ask why the passage says man and woman if it means husband and wife? The Greek uses just one word for either "man" or "husband" and one word for "woman" or "wife." Even though most instances of wife or husband are marked by a pronoun or article, many places in Scripture do not have either, yet still mean a spouse of the respective gender.[16] What determines how each word is translated is the surrounding context where that word is found.[17] A careful look at I Timothy 2:8–15 shows that "husband and wife" is a perfect translation in this passage, given the immediate context of Paul's subject of proper order in the world (2:1–7), in the home (2:8–15), and in the church (3:1–15).[18]

Look again at the parallels of this passage to I Peter 3:1–6.[19] Both passages deal with similar concepts of wives learning modesty and a quiet spirit and the husbands praying with right attitudes.[20] Paul and Peter use many of the same ideas in these parallel passages:

I Peter 3	**I Timothy 2**
Appearance (v. 3)	Appearance (v. 9)
Behavior (v. 4)	Behavior (v. 9)
Submissiveness (v. 5)	Submissiveness (v. 11)
How not to talk to the man (v. 1, 2)	How not to talk to the man (v. 12)
An Old Testament wife (v. 6)	An Old Testament wife (v. 13)
A quiet spirit (v. 4)	A quiet spirit (v. 11, 12)[21]

In his writing, Peter emphasized that the wives win their husbands to the Lord not by speaking but by living a humble, holy life. Paul also told the wives to submit and not control the husbands by what they were teaching. Paul presented Eve as a negative role model while Peter called Sarah a positive example of a good wife.[22]

The call for submission in I Timothy 2:11 makes it clear that this passage must apply to wives. God does not call women to submit to men at random but to submit to their own men, their husbands (as in Ephesians 5:22). Paul moved forward in verses 13–14 talking about Adam and Eve and referred to her as "his woman," which of course is translated as "his wife." Finally, verse 15 mentions childbirth, which is not a church role but a function by a wife.[23]

Therefore, one translation gives this possible rendering:

> "A *wife* should learn in quietness and full submission. I do not permit a *wife* to teach or to assume authority *over her husband*." [24]

Such an understanding of this passage stays in complete harmony with the rest of the Word of God where teachings for husbands and wives emphasize that they are to walk in peace and unity. There is a subtle shade of meaning to the word translated "authority" or "have dominion"[25] that could indicate a type of violence or at the very least bullying. Yes, it would not be proper for a woman to bully her husband.[26]

Since these verses do not reference the church, we should let them speak to a woman's proper role in the home. Otherwise, women everywhere will have to stay silent, not teach (in schools or anywhere else), and not have authority over men (even if they own a business or join the workforce). This is certainly not what Paul meant, but if one makes certain assumptions based on this verse, that is where they must lead. Paul does not address behavior in the church until chapter 3.

Sarah stood against bad influences in her home and *taught* Abraham that it would be best for the slave and her child to leave. Some would say this woman was out of her place to tell her husband what he should do. Instead, the Lord told him, "Whatever Sarah has said to you, listen to her voice."[27] So, the problem is not a wife teaching, but any destructive kind of teaching.

My wife taught me how to sing and coached me in doing some vocal harmony. As a personal trainer and health coach, she has educated me on how to properly manage the human body. It was not a violation of Scripture for my wife to teach me. It would stretch this verse too much to say that it means a woman cannot teach her husband. She simply should not speak things that tear him down.[28]

CORRECTING FALSE PERCEPTIONS

The ideologies of the female goddess cults of Ephesus and that Anatolian region may have influenced women to push a specific myth from these local pagan religions. There are hints of this in Paul's statements[29] and in the local culture.[30] Ephesian women grew up under the influence of Artemis whose followers were militant, exemplified by their feverous chanting "Great is Artemis of the Ephesians."[31]

Of a variety of goddesses in the region, Artemis was the most popular. She was believed to be the child of Leto and Zeus. She never married because of the severity of her mother's labor, says the legend. She did have a male consort but her religion made her and all her female devotees superior to men.[32] When Paul mentions fighting with "*beasts at Ephesus*"[33] he probably is referring to the struggle he faced against the followers of Artemis in Ephesus, also known as "Queen of the Wild *Beasts*."[34] The man who faced being torn to shreds by the people of Ephesus[35] says, "Let a woman learn calmly."[36]

"For Adam was formed first, then Eve"
After addressing spousal conflict, I Timothy 2:13 goes on to say, "For Adam was formed first, then Eve." We cannot make this passage say that since a man was created first, a woman cannot teach. That is too much of a jump of logic, especially when Jesus said, "The last will be first."[37] Verse 13 is not about gender superiority or subjugation of the woman.

Verse 13 corrects the Ephesians' ideas about gender roles. In their mythology, Artemis (female) was born before her brother Apollo (male). However, the true story of divine order was Adam (male) before Eve (female). Where the local pagans put great emphasis on the woman being first, the new believers would need these foundational teachings to undo the lies they grew up with.[38] Female goddesses had been considered the authors of life in that region because of their giving birth.[39] Paul recaps that the true beginning was the man in Genesis, not a woman.

Also, Paul may have emphasized the true story of human origins in response to a budding form of Gnosticism which reversed the created order, making Eve superior. He speaks out against things which are "falsely called knowledge" in 6:20 which uses the Greek word *gnosis*, that might have referred to an early form of Gnosticism. So then, 2:13–14 may have been a phrase-by-phrase rebuttal of false beliefs the

> *Against Ephesian mythology of the woman coming before the man, Paul revisits the true creation account.*

church was facing at the time.[40] Having come from such role-reversed backgrounds, the women needed all the teaching they could get to have a proper view of married order.

"Adam was not deceived"

If we use these statements regarding Eve to condemn women, we should also use the verses about Adam being guilty for bringing sin to everyone as a reason to indict all men.[41] However, "Adam was not deceived" but "not because he was able to see through the deception but because the serpent did not attempt to deceive him."[42] For Paul, Eve was not indicative of all women any more than Adam's sin proved that men would be more likely to sin willfully.[43]

Neither is this about men being more resistant to deception. One does not have to look far to find men who have been deceived and men who have deceived others with false doctrine. Verse 14 cannot be about gender qualifications for ministry. Men and women with equal opportunities to learn God's Word do as well as each other in understanding truth and passing it on. The two named deceivers in Ephesus were men.[44] Paul had even prophesied that males would come into that church to do damage.[45]

"but the woman being deceived"

Some Reformed (Calvinistic) theologians believe "the deception of Eve by the serpent points toward an inherent character in women generally that makes them less fitted than men to preserving the doctrinal purity of the church."[46] In contrast, a proponent of women in ministry says the meaning of this passage "is simply that Eve was not immune to temptation."[47]

If women were more vulnerable to deception, how could a woman then be trusted in matters of the faith at all? If she is so unstable, how can she teach children who are more gullible than grown men? Can she be trusted with teaching her own children or with any type of soul-winning? Why would the Lord give women prophecies and commission them to share His story? Why would Paul tell Titus that women should teach?[48]

In other writings, Paul did not see gullibility as a female trait; he worried that a whole church could be deceived like Eve was.[49] The same deceiver comes around today, not as a serpent but as an angel of light.[50] We simply cannot conclude that women cannot teach because Eve was deceived.

This "Eve was deceived" talk may have been targeting pre-Gnostic heresies, a few of which exalted Eve as the one who enlightened Adam.[51] If the women in Ephesus did not learn the truth, they would be deceived just as was Eve. These Scripture verses appear to be speaking not to women in ministry but to wives in the context of contemporary concerns. These principles still apply.

"fell into transgression"

How does it follow logically that a woman who was deceived should be somehow inferior to a man who sinned willfully? Adam was standing by while his wife ate the fruit and still he joined her in that sin (Genesis 3:6). Eve said, "The serpent deceived me, and I ate" (3:13); Adam said, "The woman… gave me of the tree, and I ate." (3:12). In other words, Adam sinned knowing full well what would happen, while the woman sinned only because she got fast-talked into it. That does not raise my trust in men being superior spiritual leaders!

Paul does not mean women are inferior. In Genesis 1:28, the Lord gave the man and the woman authority together over the earth. Can women not even teach other women? If women are morally unstable, that would be like the blind leading the blind. Paul did not think women were gullible.

Apparently the point of mentioning Eve's deception and their falling into sin together was to remind the Ephesian women that their gender was not superior as they had been taught in their religions (and as modern feminism seems to express). Eve swallowed a lie and then Adam consumed it, too. If the Ephesian women did not settle down and learn truth, they might similarly mislead their husbands. Paul did not make a universal statement about women here but a simple point to those in Ephesus that they should not repeat history.[52]

"Nevertheless she will be saved in childbearing"
Verse 14 leads into verse 15 by letting us know things got worse before they improved.[53] Again, the Artemis cult may have been the target of this statement. Artemis was not only a goddess of fertility, but she was the mythical being to whom devotees prayed during childbirth. According to the legend, immediately after her own birth, "Artemis helped her younger twin brother Apollo to be born into the world. . . For this reason, the maiden-goddess Artemis was invoked by women during labor."[54] Perhaps Paul was letting them know they did not need to depend on a superstition to survive labor or fear being punished by the goddess during delivery.[55] Enter Christ, exit Artemis. The old beliefs had no control over the new believers.

"if they continue in faith, love, and holiness, with self-control"
Rather than trying to "wear the pants in the family" these women could accept their created role in the home and thrive in it. Such qualities will not exist in a home where a woman is doing verbal violence to her husband, nor where the man is full of anger, arguments, and doubt. In summary, I Timothy 2:11–15 speaks to the proper order of modesty and godly submission of wives. They are not to teach their husbands in an effort to destroy or control them. They are to understand their role in the context of the creation story: being team-partners with their husbands, and raising a holy, loving family that continues in faith and self-control.

APPLYING THE PRINCIPLE

One key to understanding Scripture is to first grasp who was the intended audience. Once we know how the original hearers were likely to have received the message, then we can apply the same principles to our lives.[56] The original hearers understood this passage applied to married couples. The problem many make with interpreting this passage is taking it to mean that women in general must be in subjection to all men (which is impossible). Instead, a wife should not manipulate or connive to overthrow the leadership of her husband. If he is unsaved, she should not lecture him. The disputes revolving around I Timothy 2:12 would not be so many if we understood it like Charles Williams in his translation of the New Testament:

> I do not permit a married woman
> To practice teaching or domineering
> Over a husband.[57]

We should not interpret I Timothy 2:11–12 to say a woman cannot have authority at church because this is neither how the early believers understood the passage nor is it the principle behind what it says grammatically or contextually.

Sarah did much to preserve the faith in her family. She understood that modesty applied to more than her wardrobe but also her attitude. What woman could ask for more than Sarah's heritage? Even three thousand years after her time, her descendants have championed the message of the One True God. What a great accomplishment! Such a woman must teach and lead wisely. Surely she did, for Hebrews 11:11 records her as one of the elders in the hall of faith. May every believing woman be a daughter of Sarah.

7 | He Called Esther: Women in Authority

Can a woman have authority in the church?

> *And on the second day, at the banquet of wine, the king again said to Esther, "What is your petition, Queen Esther? It shall be granted you. And what is your request, up to half the kingdom? It shall be done!" (Esther 7:2).*

When young Hadassah questioned what to do when the lives of God's people were threatened, her uncle Mordecai urged her to take initiative. He said, "Who knows whether you have come to the kingdom for such a time as this?"[1] At that moment, the queen of Persia purposed in her heart to do all she could for the Lord even at the risk of her life. God raised up this woman to serve Him as a governmental leader.

> *Who knows whether you have come to the kingdom for such a time as this?*

With Deborah, we saw that God used a woman as a leader in His kingdom. With Esther, we see a woman with civic and governmental authority for God's cause. Esther was not just a woman working a job with societal authority but a queen with spiritual authority as well. What gave her access to using the rule of government in favor of God's people was her prayer and fasting along with others who understood the principle of "we wrestle not against flesh and blood."

Some opponents have claimed that a woman might be able to preach or teach but she should not have any authority. In the previous chapter we considered I Timothy 2:12 with the phrase "take authority" or "usurp authority." However, this word translated "authority" comes from an enigmatic Greek word which has garnered much discussion. Paul could have chosen a dozen others words to say "authority" if that were what he meant. He could also have chosen one out of over forty words indicating "rule" or "govern," had either of those been the meaning he intended. Paul chose the word he did because it was suited to a particular situation in Ephesus. Regarding this verse being translated as "authority," one must note that "there is no instance of this meaning in the Greek of Paul's day, and no version until Martin Luther in 1522 translates it this way."[2] However, this discussion hinges on more than just one word.

The previous chapter showed that the context of the passage is based on the relationship between a wife and her husband. We turn now to look at the biblical perspective on authority. The Bible does not use the word authority in reference to believers controlling the lives of other believers. Jesus came with the authority to heal and to command disease to leave.[3] Jesus did not use the word authority in reference to a hierarchy among His followers or within the church. Typically, secular rulers and religious bureaucrats sought authority over others.[4] Simon Magus wanted authority from the apostles,[5] and the unconverted Saul had authority to take people hostage.[6] The devil tempted Christ to take authority over all the nations of the world.[7] These forms of taking power over people stand in contrast to godly leadership.

A governmental figure rules over individuals and can control their lives to some extent. God's people should *lord over* the earth—controlling and managing plant and animal life. However, it is improper to exert that kind of control over other people. Jesus said,

> You know that the rulers of the Gentiles lord it over them, and those who are great exercise authority over them. Yet it shall not be so among you; but whoever desires to become great among you, let him be your servant. And whoever desires to be first among you, let him be your slave --- just as the Son of Man did not come to be served, but to serve, and to give His life a ransom for many (Matthew 20:25–28).

Queen Esther understood authority from a higher kingdom. It has been said that the way to the throne room is through the servant's quarters. She humbled herself and the Lord gave her favor.

Jesus contrasts control-type of authority against the servant spirit of His kingdom. He calls believers to serve one another, not manipulate each other. Jesus gave His followers authority over the powers of disease, death, and demons, but not over people.[8] Jesus had absolute power over everything but He led people and served them. Some followed at their own will. Powerful things happen when people respond to pastors and preachers of their own free will. Paul illustrated that church leaders work as a team for the followers' joy.[9]

A servant of God must command people in the Lord. Since the Word of God is our authority, we submit to those who give such instructions.[10] A male has no inherent power over others because he is male. If a woman can be a servant-leader, she can be a church leader. All believers in any position are to servant-lead and set an example for others to follow. Command-obedience relationships do away with the love and trust that grows in a voluntary submission system as the church is to be. Hierarchical imperialism creates a non-relational connection between individuals.[11]

ABSOLUTE POWER CORRUPTS

At Esther's second banquet, her husband the king said, "What is your petition, Queen Esther? It shall be granted you. And what is your request, up to half the kingdom? It shall be done!" Centuries later, another young woman came before a king who gave the same offer. King Herod observed the daughter of his new wife dancing and told her, "Whatever you ask me, I will give you, up to half my kingdom" (Mark 6:23). She followed the malicious desires of her mother Herodias and requested the murder of John the Baptist. Where one young woman used her "up to half the kingdom" opportunity as a chance to destroy the man God called, Esther used her opportunity to protect and preserve the people He had called.

The spirit of rebellion contrasts clearly against true spiritual authority. The spirit of rebellion appears in another queen. Queen Jezebel was a vicious woman who sought to destroy God's anointed ministers. Too many people today have allowed the spirit of Jezebel, a manipulative spirit of rebellion, to infiltrate their lives.

Jesus called Jezebel to repent from her perverse teaching in the church in Thyatira.[12] Some have claimed that the problem here was a woman teacher. However, Jesus did not take issue with her gender but her agenda.[13] A spirit of Jezebel works against the anointing.[14] This spirit of insubordination and conflict tries to usurp authority against a pastor or other spiritual leader. Anointing, the empowering work of the Spirit, does not flow through an attitude of self-assertiveness but through a humble, broken spirit.

> *Jesus did not take issue with Jezebel's gender but her agenda.*

Domineering women can do much damage. One prominent missionary lamented to me how a manipulative woman hurt the chances for other female ministers among the churches in the country where he had served. A pastor's wife told my wife, "I guess it's okay for a woman to preach, but I have seen some women preachers that were so domineering that it turned me off." My wife replied, "True, but I've seen domineering male preachers, too, but that didn't turn me off to men in the pulpit." Her friend agreed.

Somehow it seems a man can get away with being domineering but if a woman preacher acts wrongly, it might cast a dark shadow on other woman preachers. Some cultural contexts accept a belligerent male leader. If a woman leader has the same character flaws, some will criticize her for being unladylike and "too masculine." Despotism is not masculine, however, but impish and worldly.

THE SECOND ANOINTING

It is not enough for someone to have the call of God on her life. David had an anointing from God to be king, but he did not become one until the people of Hebron anointed him as king. Later, the whole nation accepted him and his calling came into full action. Many today who are anointed by God for ministry fail to wait on the anointing from the people.

Paul also had a call to a life of ministry, but the people in Jerusalem did not recognize it. Since he had so intensely persecuted the church, they may have worried that his conversion was not legit. In fact, they seemed quite relieved when he left their coasts.[15] Barnabas, however, took him in and gave him a place to follow his calling. You can be a Barnabas to a Paul or a Mordecai to an Esther. Whom will you help get started in his or her calling?

Those who say women can serve in the church but the leaders must be men pervert what Jesus said. He told us that if someone is to lead, they must serve. Servants are those in preparation to lead. If we accept women who serve in the Kingdom, we must also accept them as leaders. Gentlemen, we must not fight against God by discouraging women from being what He has called them to be. I cannot imagine what a frustrated person I would be today if someone had not assisted me and even challenged me to follow God's call on my life.

Churches need to encourage young women to find their place in serving the Lord, says one Apostolic woman:

> I believe it is essential that the pastor is the first and greatest supporter of young women in ministry in the church. I beg pastors to listen to these women, create opportunities for them, and invest in the ministry God is developing. The treasure you pour into them will undoubtedly return eternal results for the kingdom of God.
>
> It is God who calls and equips all of us for any type of ministry. However, as young women who are called, we have a responsibility to act upon that calling. The two greatest obstacles I have seen young women struggle with are fear and lack of opportunity or support. Fear can come from a number of sources. Fear of being misunderstood by friends, fear of being rejected by peers, and fear of not fulfilling the purpose we have been given. These fears are all very real and if not dealt with, can destroy us. As young women, it is easy to allow these fears to overcome us and ultimately claim our calling. However, there is only one true way to overcome these fears: prayer. When we find the security of our calling in God alone, external threats will no longer be able to control and paralyze us. It is God who called us and it is God who will give us the strength to fulfill that calling and to overcome any obstacles that we will face. It is also our responsibility as young women to stay submitted to the authority and leadership in our life. [16]

If you are a leader who is reticent to support young women in ministry, remember that Jezebels should not ruin it for women in ministry any more than Esthers prove that every young woman should be queen.

Just because some preacher turns out to be a lemon, people do not say, "See if we let another man be a preacher again." However, if it is a woman or a person in a racial minority for example, those in charge are quicker to throw that whole group under the bus. A headstrong woman should not be able to sour ministry for all women. At the same time, a woman should be extra careful in an atmosphere that is still not settled with the idea of female leadership.

Perhaps I am talking to the men more when I say we must guard against becoming lords of God's church. A man can get away with being a bully a lot better than a woman. People take less offense at a man who is "large and in charge" because culturally it does not look so bad. If the model in the pulpit is humility and a heart of service, more Elijahs and Elishas will arise. Leaders who ignore another's calling because of inconvenience or prejudice are playing with people's lives.

Humility is the starting point of ministry. The key point is that we are called to serve, not called to be in charge or be out front. When I think of a great leader, I do not think of great orators I have seen. I think of men like James Kilgore and women like Nona Freeman who demonstrated humility in all they did. Their eyes did not glisten from the bright lights but from the care they had for others. Frank Ewart emphasized the humble heart:

> This is true of all God's great servants. In their God-given humility lay the basis of their power and influence. When one vanished, the other diminished and slowly died out. . . .
>
> When Alexander Dowie lost his humility he lost his power to heal the people, and God ceased to commit Himself to him. . . .
>
> All the great leaders . . . sat at the feet of the Master long enough to learn this great secret of power. . . .
>
> All the great men of God—great in ratio as they were humble—would simply guide the worship in the Spirit so that God could get the very highest glory out of each meeting. . . .
>
> Point me out the men in this movement whom God delighteth to honor, from Brother W. J. Seymour to the great leaders of the present day, and I will show

you men who realize that their greatest asset is a God-given humility.[17]

As a quote attributed to Margaret Thatcher says, "Being powerful is like being a lady. If you have to tell people you are, you aren't."

> *Being powerful is like being a lady. If you have to tell people you are, you aren't.*

Servant-leadership operates with the power of humility that is lacking in carnal institutions. When I look in the courtrooms, I do not see many judges who are humble. In the halls of our national leaders, I see a smugness that many admire in those who lead the greatest country on earth. However, the church is not a branch of the military where we boast of how much better we are than others. We follow the one who let them mock Him and kill Him.

BIBLICAL SUBMISSION

I am a firm believer in the power of submission. In the kingdom of God, the authority to which we submit is God and His Word. A minister is a servant under authority who conveys the Master's commands. Those who oppose the servant oppose the Master. The servant, however, does not have the right to make up rules and demand that others comply.

Once I pulled out of an attempt to start a new church, even though I was sure God had called me to start a work in that rural area. My wife and I agreed that God had called us, doors had opened for us to have a home there, and a community group offered us free use of a church building. However, I believe so strongly that a child of God must walk in submission, that I would not go against those servants of the Lord to whom I am submitted.[18]

Someone might argue, "I don't think another person has a right to tell you what you can or cannot do for God." Such a one should revisit the story of when Jesus submitted Himself to Mary and Joseph. Moses finally could lead the

Hebrews once the elders of Israel accepted him as a man sent from God. The blessings of God and opportunities to serve Him have overwhelmed me after I submitted to my leadership.

The kingdom of God is not about who has the authority over others; it is about who is willing to submit to someone who technically has no control over you.[19] It appears that Lucile Farmer learned this principle:

> Brother Vouga said to me, "Sister Farmer, I know you are interested in the work down in the middle of the jungles, but you must come back to Quito. This is the capital. We have to establish a strong work here before we can branch out into other places. I want you to work here in Quito until this work grows; then we can think about going out into other places."
>
> I was somewhat disappointed about these instructions because Brother Limones in Quito had difficulty in accepting me as his missionary supervisor. They all highly respected me, were kind to me, and treated me as a member of the family, but because I was a woman, he could not accept me as his supervisor. As a result, I did not know how I was going to work with Brother Limones. He was a man of prayer, a good pastor and an especially good evangelist, but I did not know how we would work together. The Lord worked the situation out later, so the move was for the best, after all.[20]

A powerful miracle of healing soon followed in Lucile's life.

A person will not advance in his or her calling until he or she submits to leaders in the kingdom of God. Submission accepts someone who serves God as being a representative of His authority although that leading individual has no ability to execute physical judgment (as could a governmental leader). The authority in the minister's life is the Word of God. When people oppose that, judgment is clear: you will not enter the Kingdom. This is not a person's decision but

God's. The minister/servant simply relays that message for Him.

I am eager to submit myself to those who lead the body of Christ; I must also take care how I lead others. The Word tells the believer to be submissive to "those who rule over you" and indicates that this is for the followers' own good (Hebrews 13:17). At the same time, those in leadership cannot make arbitrary decisions that manipulate the content and quality of others' lives. The same chapter explains submission to "those who rule over you, who have spoken the word of God to you" (13:7). Believers submit to leaders in the church because they are speaking the Word of God. Ultimately, the pastor's authority is God's Word. Therefore, whether a man, woman, or child speaks God's Word, the hearers are obligated to obey its message.

When a person submits to a pastor, he or she begins to understand how upside down the kingdom of God is compared to the rest of the world. When people choose to walk in submission, they find great power in God. When individuals choose to try to control others or exercise authority, they come up empty and frustrated. We do not have the opportunity to take charge; we are given the opportunity to lay down our lives. Blessings come to those who submit.

Thank God that Apollos submitted himself to the teaching of Priscilla and Aquila. Thank God that Timothy listened to Lois and Eunice. How amazing that Jesus listened to Mary at the wedding feast in Cana. What a man of God Josiah was that he would submit himself to the word of the Lord that came from Huldah the prophetess. How refreshing it was that the eleven apostles submitted themselves to the word of the Lord delivered by the women who had been to the tomb. What a blessing it was for Samaria that the men of the city submitted to the instructions of the woman who told them to come meet Jesus, and they met Him for themselves. How blessed I have been by reading the writings of women of God and how life changing it has been for me to submit myself to the preaching of women of God.

Some men become very defensive at the thought of submitting to a women leader. I wish the man who says a woman cannot have authority would tell the female officer standing at his window that she has no jurisdiction over him. Afterward, he would have a chance to tell the female judge that her ruling is of no consequence because a woman really does not have authority. Haman found out too late not to mess with a woman in authority. Does a Christian man not have to listen to his female supervisor in the workplace? These are examples of secular authority; in God's kingdom, how much more respect should we have for a woman when the authority is His?

SACRIFICIAL AUTHORITY

Imagine a rebellious college student who wanted to express his right to not salute our nation's flag during the singing of the national anthem. Standing there in the crowd with his arms crossed, he refuses to put his hand on his heart. Then a policeman walks up and says, "You need to honor our flag and our country for which it stands."

"You can't make me," comes the brazen reply.

The policeman walks away because the young man is right. No one can make a person honor our country and those who have sacrificed for us.

Cold-hearted, the youth continues to stand there, staring into the distance, jaw set, proud of his insolence. Then someone steps up and clears his throat. He turns to see an old man looking him in the eye. His left arm is missing. On his shirt there are a few metals and a purple heart. In his hand he holds a hat that says, "Veteran." He struggles to speak and then says, "Would you please respect my flag. I gave everything for her."

Whether he changes the student's opinions or his rebellious ways or not, even a cold heart could not resist such a request. He nods, saying nothing, and puts his hand on his heart while the anthem continues. What motivated him was not someone in control but someone who had sacrificed. What broke his pride was broken humility. Power in the church is not the control-type of power a policeman wields but the respect we have for those who have given all.

The rank one attains in God's army is not like corporal or commander; it is more like the honor deserved by war veterans. The Purple Heart rewards military men who risked it all. Another illustration would be if one child rescues another from drowning, she receives greater honor and attention not because she is intrinsically better than other children but because she went beyond for a cause greater than self. In the church, those who serve with all their hearts and give themselves tirelessly to the Kingdom become our heroes—the ones who naturally rise in leadership.

In Pentecostal circles, we usually give credence to those who have had most impact in building the Kingdom (soul-winning) and whose ministries have been confirmed with miracles. This is not hierarchy but natural leadership. Occasionally in organizational politics, those with natural leadership abilities get voted into key positions. The first point of recognition for any leader is that person's calling. Paul often used two credentials as reasons why anyone should listen to him: his calling and his level of sacrifice.[21]

The elders of the church do not hold a sword like the governmental authorities. Pastors are not in a kingship. Believers submit to leaders out of love and respect because they are our veterans. It was their sacrifice that brought us the gospel. The great leader did not use bully power but led by humility: "for love's sake I rather appeal to you—being such a one as Paul, the aged, and now also a prisoner of Jesus Christ" (Philemon 9). He asked for compliance not because of how high his rank was, but based on how low he had stooped to further the gospel.

Yes, the flock does submit to the shepherd, but we submit out of respect for someone who has humbled himself or herself to serve. We honor those who tend to our spiritual needs "just as a nursing mother cherishes her own children." And we listen to and obey those who exhort us "as a father does his own children" (I Thessalonians 2:7, 11). Church leadership draws on both mothering and fatherhood qualities. Any church leader today, male or female, must follow this spirit. Rather than seeking recognition, one must serve as a devoted mother and committed father. Rather than take advantage or abuse the role, one must give themselves for the care and growth of the believers.

Postmodern individuals will be quick to say, "Nobody is better than me. We are all equal." Although we are all of equal value, the Lord calls us to love others as if they were of higher value than ourselves. Too many balk at the idea of submission because it sounds too much like a dictatorship.

> Our objections, whether philosophical or emotional, to this hierarchical system arise because we do not know what a sinless hierarchy is like. We know only the tyranny, willfulness and condescension that even the best boss-underling relationship has.[22]

Rather than look at rank, we look at one's labor of love. You are to "recognize those who labor among you, and are over you in the Lord and admonish you, and to esteem them very highly in love for their work's sake."

When you learn to honor those in leadership, you are on the path to being a leader. Rather than looking for a chance to be in charge, look for people to serve in the

Lord. Serve Him first and the people as a result of that. Such servant-leadership will never lack a place to serve for those who will respectfully submit.

Who is to say but that a woman reading this book has been called for such a time as this!

8 | He Called Phoebe: Women as Ministers

Can a woman be a licensed/ordained minister?

> *I commend to you Phoebe our sister, who is a servant of the church in Cenchrea, that you may receive her in the Lord in a manner worthy of the saints, and assist her in whatever business she has need of you; for indeed she has been a helper of many and of myself also*
> *(Romans 16:1–2).*

Paul called Phoebe a patroness. When Paul had to return to Jerusalem with a special offering, He sent his letter with Phoebe to the believers at Rome. She was his patroness in the sense of financially and logistically supporting his travels to the West. Her patronage may be what supported him when he traveled to Rome in chains. It may also have been her money that provided him a house in Rome.[1]

Phoebe was a sponsor of many, not just Paul.[2] *Thayer's Dictionary* says the word *prostatis* can mean "a woman set over others" or "a female guardian, protectress, patroness, caring for the affairs of others and aiding them with her resources." Many Bible translations often downgrade this word to "helper" as if she could only assist rather than lead on her own. However, Paul used this word in its verb form clearly to distinguish those in church leadership.[3]

Phoebe's ministry calling appears to have been the gift of leading[4] and therefore Paul has asked her to carry his systematic theology (the Epistle to the Romans) as his representative. Phoebe went before Paul to arrange his accommodations and possibly collect resources as well as personnel for his missionary campaign. Remarkably, Paul turned down financial support from the Corinthian church, but received support from this donor as he did from Lydia in Philippi.[5] Jesus also had many female patronesses. In fact, rich men are usually cast in a negative light in Scripture, but rich women are often presented in a positive light. In addition to several historical instances of female Jewish donors, we find New Testament instances of women patrons as well.[6]

Paul trusted this leader of the congregation[7] in Cenchrea, a port near Corinth, to represent him before a community of Christians he had not met yet. Part of her job might have been going before him to handpick a missions team to travel with him to Spain.[8] The fellow-laborers he mentions in Romans 16 may have been those he intended to help spearhead the operation.

Whatever the details regarding this influential woman, obviously Paul trusted Phoebe to read his letter and present some weighty doctrinal teaching to a distant body of believers. Some of them would not know the apostle and would have questions about the things he said. She would have to stand in for Paul and represent him in how she responded to these questions.

Paul had trusted other agents to represent him: Timothy in Ephesus, Titus in Crete, Epaphroditus in Philippi, Tychicus in Ephesus, and Tychicus and Onesimus together to Colosse.[9] Paul had the least familiarity with the believers in Rome so his sending Phoebe shows he had absolute trust in this woman not just to follow up like the other agents had done for him, but to pave the way for him to have a positive relationship with the Roman church from whom he would need mission partners.[10] If Paul had something against women in ministry, it was another huge oversight on his part to send a woman to present his letter!

He says, "I commend to you Phoebe our sister, who is a servant of the church in Cenchrea" (Romans 16:1). The same word translated as "minister" when used for Paul and his male teammates is translated as "servant" when used regarding a woman.[11] The literal word is deacon. It is not a feminine form of the word, such as deaconness, but Paul chose the same noun he used for men to describe Phoebe.[12] It would be wrong for Phoebe to "be called a deaconess because the masculine form of the word is used here and because the specific order of women church workers called deaconesses did not exist for another three hundred years."[13] This word tells us "Phoebe was clearly a leader, and most likely *the* leader (minister) of the new church in that harbor town near Corinth."[14]

> *"Phoebe was clearly a leader, and most likely the leader (minister) of the new church in that harbor town near Corinth."*
> *– Kenneth Bailey*

JESUS WAS A DEACON

Deacon has a different cultural meaning in most modern contexts than it did in the first-century church. Denominations today might call church board members deacons or use this term to designate lay leaders in the church. The Greek word can mean "deacon," "servant," or "minister."[15] I prefer to use the word *minister* since most Pentecostal churches do not designate a title of deacon, but we all understand what a minister is.

Jesus said He came to serve (minister), not to be served.[16] The first event in Christianity to use these terms was when the apostles appointed seven men to minister to women, the

Hellenistic widows.[17] Perhaps we could consider these ministers in training because not only were they taking care of administrative details (serving tables may have meant managing resources for the widows) but they later serve the Word along with the apostles and elders. Stephen and Philip became remarkable evangelists and fiery preachers.

This might help explain the differentiation between "bishops and deacons" or "overseers and ministers" in Paul's writings. The overseers were seasoned in the ministry while the ministers were developing maturity in the work of the Lord.[18] The twelve apostles had been ministers in training under the Lord for three and a half years before taking leadership roles. It has long been popular in Pentecost that the path to the pulpit comes by way of cleaning the commodes. Those who will not wash others' feet will not do well serving the gospel either.

Minister describes all workers in the Kingdom, including apostles and evangelists.[19] While a person would always be a minister, his or her ministry gifts may focus on teaching, church planting, or other specialties that grow with time.[20] The servant-then-leader sequence of development modeled Jesus' statement that one qualified to lead by first being servant of all. Here is how the apostle explained this important role in the church:

> Likewise deacons [ministers] must be reverent, not double-tongued, not given to much wine, not greedy for money, holding the mystery of the faith with a pure conscience. But let these also first be tested; then let them serve as deacons [ministers], being found blameless. Likewise, their wives must be reverent, not slanderers, temperate, faithful in all things. Let deacons [ministers] be the husbands of one wife, ruling their children and their own houses well. For those who have served well as deacons [ministers] obtain for themselves a good standing and great boldness in the faith which is in Christ Jesus (I Timothy 3:8-13).

This list follows the character description of the bishops (overseers), which is discussed in the next chapter. Many expectations are the same between the two groups. The distinction in roles may simply be that the overseer would be training and developing ministers.

WOMEN WERE DEACONS

In this passage discussing ministers, it is interesting that some translators assume that a minister can only be male. They make the judgment call of making the passage say, "Likewise, their wives. . . ." Again, this word for "wife" is the same word translated as "woman" depending on the context.[21] In fact, the word "their" does not even exist in the original text of this passage. This text is directed toward female ministers, not simply ministers' wives. Clement of Alexandria understood the passage this way: "We know what the honorable Paul in one of his letters to Timothy prescribed regarding women deacons."[22]

This is not a group apart from the ministers, but to women within the group, also called ministers in their own right, with some specific character expectations for them as well.[23] It might be this same grouping of ministers that John referred to as "young people"[24] and Paul called "young men" and "young women" when giving similar instructions to Titus.[25] Rather than the strict structural order of "bishop and deacon" modernism celebrated, these ministers might be more in line with the "every member is a minister" campaigns of recent history.[26] However, the expectations of those called minister are high and it is clear that Paul did not use this term flippantly for every attendee, even though all believers should serve in some capacity.

After mentioning women, Paul spoke again of ministers in general, saying, "Let deacons be the husbands of one wife" (3:12). Divorce was a major issue in Greek society then as it is now.[27] Paul did not refer to men only on this issue, but later when speaking to women only, he mentioned a godly woman has been "wife of one husband" as well.[28]

It is interesting that in the subsection addressing the women, the label "wife of one husband" is absent. Surely this moral character quality applied to women as much as men. Regardless of whether one reads this as "female ministers" or "ministers' wives" the moral quality of faithfulness in marriage would still be expected. However, as discussed in the next chapter more thoroughly, such a statement said in the masculine form applied equally to both genders. Yes, men and women need to be faithful in marriage to be servants of God. The "likewise" lets us know to expect strong morals from both male and female workers in the church.

The weight of responsibility he gave to those he called ministers and coworkers was heavy indeed. By calling Phoebe a minister, Paul indicated that she measured up to the high expectations of the gospel and had proved herself in service and leadership. To call Phoebe servant and helper is insufficient. She should rightfully be designated as minister and chief supporter of the gospel. Philip, one of the early ministers of the church, not only preached the gospel but also baptized the new believers.[29] Phoebe and other women ministers then would be on the same level of commitment and responsibility and therefore able to baptize others as well. A secular report at the beginning of the second century speaks of Christian slave-women who were ministers.[30] In the fifth century, Pelagius reported that women both preached and administered baptisms in his day.[31] Nothing in the Scriptures forbids a woman this right and responsibility of those who go into all the world making disciples.[32]

> *By calling Phoebe a minister, Paul indicated that she measured up to the high expectations of the gospel and had proved herself in service and leadership.*

The focus is not so much on whether we call a woman deacon, minister, or something else. The key is that believers recognize that God calls women, even as He dramatically did with Opal Blackford:

> As she sat at her machine one day, Opal heard a very soft voice calling her name. She turned to the lady sitting next to her and asked what she wanted. The lady was quite surprised and said that she had not called Opal's name.
> Opal began to work again, only to have the same experience. The voice called very gently, "Opal."
> When she heard the voice the second time, Opal began to cry. On the second calling she had recognized the voice from God. For several months since the twins were born, she had felt God calling her to preach. Now she knew that this sweet voice was one more call from the Lord.
> The elderly lady sitting at the next machine ran to Opal. "What's wrong little girl? Are you about to have a holy roller's fit?"
> The women about her began to chide her and one said, "Don't you know that crying makes your skin wrinkle?"
> Her only reply was to God. "Please, Lord, make me a wrinkled persimmon, if that is what it will take for me to be a soul winner."[33]

WOMEN FINDING A PLACE TO WORK

Men often reference the written Christian works of women in their sermons or teach Bible lessons written by women. I cannot imagine how it could be okay for a woman to write gospel truth but not speak it. Unfortunately, "the gospel is hindered by an unnecessary prohibition on women's ministry" when the church "would in fact be helped by encouraging it."[34] The leadership gifts in the church prepare and equip the believers to do the work of the ministry (Ephesians 4:12). Knowing this and realizing that women are called to these roles, we should stop limiting our growth and let those who are called lead. "The church has a vast reservoir of talent in her devoted and highly qualified women. To keep this treasure in storage is poor stewardship. It is time for the church to put to use, to the fullest extent, the mission potential she has in her women."[35]

Women ministers commonly led in the first-century church.[36] In the next century, Justin wrote about spiritually gifted men and women working in the church. Also in the second century, the martyr Perpetua influenced many with her writings, and Sophia was another Phoebe, a minister and "virgin of Christ."[37] Origen, in the third century, said that Paul's endorsement of Phoebe "teaches with the authority of the apostle that even women are instituted deacons in the church." In the fourth century, John Chrysostom said that Paul specified "her rank by calling her a deacon" and spoke "of women who held the rank of deacon in the apostolic church."[38]

If a woman cannot find acceptance in the local church, she might find her place of usefulness in starting a daughter work or church plant in cooperation with her leadership. The world already does business with female bosses, professors, senators, governors, police, and doctors. People in some cultures would not be shocked to have a woman minister in their lives. In such a setting, a woman could train up and influence other men and women to serve as mentors and elders to others.

In a church plant, a woman minister could be serving as pastor to the small flock. Like Priscilla shepherding Apollos, a woman of God can raise up the next generation of truth bearers. Like the women telling the truth of the resurrection to the disciples, a woman today can proclaim He is risen, too. As Eunice and Lois passed their faith on to Timothy, so a woman can disciple men and women in righteousness. Paul did not merely say women *can* teach, but that they *should* be "teachers of good things" (Titus 2:3).

If the true church rejects women from serving in the Kingdom, some women might feel their only place of expression would be in denominations that follow a social gospel (rather than a biblically based belief system). One of the first women to be ordained in ministry, Antoinette Brown found better acceptance for her ministry among liberal theologians. It seems some denominations devoid of the moving of the Spirit accept women clergy on a civil rights agenda. Some of these same denominations even accept clergy members who have a distorted sexual self-identity.[39] We advocate for women in ministry from a scriptural context for women in ministry. There is no biblical precedent for acceptance of homosexuality or transgender leaders in the church.

Near the end of the eighteenth century, another Phoebe became an outspoken preacher. Phoebe Palmer left her mark on the early Methodist/holiness movement.[40] Walter, Phoebe's husband, supported and encouraged her ministry. She became a sought after camp-meeting preacher and revivalist leading a major revival in Ontario in 1857 followed by two significant revivals in New York.[41] Phoebe Palmer warned her ministerial contenders that repressing female ministers would hold back "the growth of the church and the coming of God's kingdom" as well as impose a heavy burden upon women.[42] She wrote that the rejection by men proved to be a "slowly crucifying process" for her but that she had managed without bitterness, knowing she was following God's call, not church tradition.

MOVING FORWARD IN MINISTRY

How do you get into ministry? Serve. This is where every God-called person starts. Want to be noticed for your calling? Do it. Are you called to preach? Then go and win souls. Are you called to teach? Then share with those who do not know the truth of God's Word. No one can argue with souls being added to the Kingdom. A woman should not depend on social recognition to feel validated. One does not need a pulpit as a place to get started in ministry.

Pentecostals originally accepted the idea of women in ministry because women preachers arose as God moved on them. We found the Bible supported this involvement once we got past our traditions. Today, women of God fulfill their callings in the global mission field, in evangelizing cities of North America, and in church planting. Such involvement will grow the church and be of direct benefit to such women of faith.[43]

How do you help others get started in ministry if you are in leadership? We can start with the language we use. For example, the cultural meaning of the word *prince* is not the same as *princess*. In popular culture, one might think of a prince as a hero and a princess as a victim in need of rescue. Paul did not call Phoebe a deaconess or a ministeress. We should not make female leaders a different subset in the church. Labels such as reverend or minister should be the same across the board for men and women.[44] To refer to a woman as "choir director" but a man with the same position as "minister of music" reveals a bias. Our congregations need to hear inclusive language that does not just say, "God is looking for a man to serve Him" but "God is looking for someone to serve Him."

There is consistency in Jesus' invitational statements; He used gender inclusive pronouns in the Greek. He was inviting any who would come. The call of God is inclusive and our word choices should reflect that. I do not expect a new believer to hear how my sermon applies to her if I only talk about how much God loves every man and how He is calling all men to work for Him. For her to hear the message, I must speak her

> *When encouraging workers in the harvest, our invitational statements should be gender inclusive.*

language of inclusivity. Sexist language could be a stumbling block to a new convert.

Ministers in training need good leaders. In Pentecost, it is usually our pastors or Bible schools that train up the next generation of ministers. As a pastor responsible for helping others find their place of service in the Kingdom, I must realize the Lord called me to serve the body, not to be the head of it. If this were about me controlling others, He would have called me a king or sovereign. Instead, a pastor must provide a pasture where others can grow to their full potential.

When a pastor catches the vision to serve the people of God by providing them a place to grow and be nourished, natural leaders arise. The shepherd is a guide to the sheep, but they have their own natural leadership that develops among them. Look at all the people Jesus trained into the Kingdom: numerous disciples who ministered farther and wider than He did. I have to ask, "Is that the model I am following in my ministry? Or am I looking to control as many as I can?" The more people pastors and leaders release to serve, the more the flock will grow.

Of course, a shepherd must be selective. Not every man or every woman who says he or she is called to ministry is going to be a fit within the local congregation. Perhaps there are moral issues to be resolved or personality clashes that may never resolve like John Mark had with Paul.[45] However, despite Paul's doubts regarding his eligibility for service, John Mark eventually became a great servant of the Lord whom Paul applauded. I cannot let my own personality clash with someone hinder what God has called him or her to be.

As pastors, we must be watchers over the souls of the flock. Too many men of God have fallen into the pit of lording over others. It is our duty to create a sending environment where more Bug and Nona Freemans can be launched forward into all God intends for them. We need to ask the Lord to help us lead individuals to their proper function in Christ.

How would you answer these questions:

> Can a woman look after the spiritual well-being of other believers?
> Can a woman share the gospel?
> Can a woman invite others to respond and obey the gospel?
> Can a woman expound insights from the Scriptures?
> Can she uplift and challenge other believers?

I imagine you, like most Pentecostal believers, would answer yes to these questions. Each of these applies to certain roles or callings in the body of Christ. If I change it to a question of "Can a woman be a pastor," does that change anything? We will give these questions further consideration in the next chapter.

9 | He Called Lydia: Women as Pastors

Can a woman be a pastor?

> *And on the Sabbath day we went out of the city to the riverside, where prayer was customarily made; and we sat down and spoke to the women who met there. Now a certain woman named Lydia heard us. She was a seller of purple from the city of Thyatira, who worshiped God. The Lord opened her heart to heed the things spoken by Paul. And when she and her household were baptized, she begged us, saying, "If you have judged me to be faithful to the Lord, come to my house and stay." So she persuaded us*
> *(Acts 16:13–15).*

In a dream, Paul saw a man calling him to go to the region of Macedonia. When he arrived in Macedonia, in the city of Philippi, he did not find a man open to the gospel. Instead, he found a woman who was ready to respond. Lydia led a women's prayer group down by the river because there was no Jewish synagogue in town where the God-fearing Gentiles could meet. Later, Paul and Silas were ministering in town and cast a demon out of a slave girl who also joined the church.

Up to this point, it does not appear that Paul had found a man who would respond to the gospel. When the evangelists were thrown into jail, Paul found his man. After God miraculously broke the chains and shook up the building, Paul and Silas were able to minister to the jailer. He came to the Lord in the dark hours of the night, along with his household, but the next morning the city leaders asked Paul to leave town.

Here is the big question: who should pastor this church? If a man must be in charge, it appears only the jailer would qualify. This means the new pastor would have only come to the faith within the past twenty-four hours! That jailer was sincere, but he was not ready to lead a church. It seems more practical to have installed Lydia as leader of the church in her home. She had already proven herself as a capable manager of a business and leader of a religious gathering in a non-religious city.

The church in Philippi included other women in leadership as well. Paul mentioned Euodia and Syntyche, two women who had been co-laborers with him in the gospel. The issue that involved these two women was so significant that Paul brought it to the attention of the church as a whole. They must have had some rank in the church because Paul appealed to Clement and another fellow-laborer of his to mediate with these women.[1]

Lydia and thousands of other women were business owners which would have made them masters over their workers, including men. Since management was not a male-only thing either in Judaism or Roman culture, by such comparison a woman could also be a leader of men and women in the church. Philippi must not have only been a place that welcomed women leaders in business but also in religion. It is possible that women would have led this church since the original converts were women, and they would have been more mature and ready to lead than any of the later converts. Perhaps Philippi was the proving ground for women to be involved in ministry as Galatia was the proving ground for including Gentiles who did not follow Moses' law.

Popular opponents against women in ministry appear to hold the view that a woman can lead and take authority in the workplace as a manager or business owner, but in the church she cannot lead. This creates a climate where churches raise young men to serve the Lord and young ladies to join the secular work force. In some ways, such thinking fuels the cause of feminism. I suggest we raise our daughters to be kingdom-minded leaders, not just mere job-hunters.

Eva Hunt pastored and planted churches funded by her husband's employment. Thomas Suey has suggested that this traditional arrangement of the husband being the income provider in the home may have been part of the reason more women were in ministry in the early Pentecostal movement. Perhaps that is why "there are not as many women in ministry today because households feel a necessity to have two-incomes."[2]

A FEMALE PASTOR?

A man stepped to the pulpit of a church pastored by a woman and said, "Well, God used a donkey so I guess He can use anybody." This woman's influence had reached far beyond his own, but all he could see was her gender.

God can call anyone.

While no one should belittle another's calling, none should think he or she is someone special due to a certain calling either. The Lord calls everyone to serve Him in some way. It is not even a matter of the success syndrome we look for. It is about doing what God has called one to do in whatever place and setting. Some plant, others water, but we must all do as the Lord leads us.

In the twentieth century, many women caught the wave of Pentecost and responded to a call to preach. Aimee Semple McPherson founded a Bible college, radio station, prayer tower, commissary, and the Angelus Temple.[3] McPherson founded the International Church of the Foursquare Gospel.

At the time of her death, 67 percent of ordained ministers in the ICFG were women.[4] Because of the bottleneck of male control in many religious institutions, many women whom God called had to build up a congregation to minister to. Such was the story of Ida Robinson who also founded a female-minister-friendly denomination.[5] Marie Burgess Brown ministered within the Pentecostal movement for over sixty years. She pastored with her husband and carried on the pastorate after his death, a ministry path many other Pentecostal widows followed as well.[6]

The pastor of the world's largest church reportedly said, "You in the West will never see a move of God until you use your women."[7] That church began in a woman's home and continues to encourage women in ministry with two-thirds of the pastoral staff being female. Perhaps *never* is too strong, but one must ponder what things would be like if there was broader acceptance of women ministers in our churches.

Is there a scriptural precedent for a woman to be a pastor? Pentecostals typically use the word pastor more than reverend or other religious titles. In the New Testament, not only will you not find a woman called pastor, but you will not find a man called pastor either. *Pastor* means "shepherd." While we use the term as an official title, it was more of a functional term. In other words, it is not something you are but something you do. A person must shepherd the sheep, leading them and caring for them. We have seen that a woman can lead and care for others, so, on that simple definition at least, she can pastor a church.

We find several biblical terms used to describe church leaders: elder, bishop, leader, and pastor.[8] Peter and Paul's use of these words indicate that in their time, these were not technical job descriptions, but interchangeable labels. Speaking to all the elders[9] in Ephesus, Paul told them to "take heed to yourselves and to all the flock, among which the Holy Spirit has made you overseers [bishops], to shepherd [pastor] the church of God which He purchased with His own blood."[10] Peter also told elders to "Shepherd [pastor] the flock of God which is among you, serving as overseers [bishops]."[11] In other words, a pastor is a bishop is an elder.

Reformed theologians have rejected the idea of women as pastors because they interpret the guideline lists as being for men only. If this is the case, we have another list of ministry gifts that needs to be edited out for women. Which of the following should we deem as unsuitable for women?

Apostles
Prophets
Evangelists
Pastors and teachers (Ephesians 4:12)

We have already seen where women fill the roles in this list of ministry giftings. Nothing about such lists or the ones we have examined previously indicate that they rule women out.

In the Pentecostal movement, we know God still speaks through His people. So, can a woman prophesy but not give a *planned* message from God as in a sermon or lesson? Since prophets speak irregular and spontaneous messages from God, the message is not dependent on the individual's contribution or personal thoughts. So, if a woman puts thought into something she says, is she disqualified from speaking for God? To say a woman can prophesy but not teach sounds like saying that women "can minister as long as they do it *without* using Scripture!"[12]

In Antioch, the prophets and teachers led the church.[13] Today, we often do not call a person by the labels the first-century church used. However, if prophets and teachers were the leaders then, would they not be the equivalent of pastors today?[14] This we do know: that God invites women to prophesy and teach. Prophets and teachers are leaders in the body of Christ. God chooses female spokespersons to represent Himself to the body.

If a person[15] desires to be an overseer of the flock, such an individual "desires a good work" (I Timothy 3:1). Who should have a heart to oversee or to look after others in the church? Everyone. Although many translations use "men" or "man" in the descriptions for church leaders, the nouns and pronouns used are never definitively masculine but are gender inclusive. Hebrews 12:15 calls all believers to be "looking carefully [overseeing][16] lest anyone fall short of the grace of God." Jesus expects believers to oversee or visit those who are sick, imprisoned, or unclothed.[17] A soulwinner is only a good soulwinner if he or she follows up with the new believer and provides spiritual care after the new birth. Just as a parent does not abandon a newborn child, so a responsible believer does not abandon a new convert. Women are natural caregivers and do a great job of looking after those who have just entered the Kingdom. Mainly, a pastor cares for the flock.

> *Who should have a heart to oversee or to look after others in the church? Everyone.*

Those who officially oversee in the church need a proven record of being those who look after others. Faithfulness in marriage, diligence in raising children, and benevolence are traits that indicate a person is prepared to steer others in the right direction. If one can lead a family well, he or she is well on the way to care for the believers.[18]

HUSBAND OF ONE WIFE

Most Pentecostals believe women can preach, but some have assumed that a woman cannot pastor because of a phrase in this passage: "A bishop then must be blameless, the husband of one wife, temperate, sober-minded, of good behavior, hospitable, able to teach…" (I Timothy 3:2). Technically, a pastor would be more akin to the minister/deacon we addressed in the previous chapter. A bishop would be an overseer of other ministers, perhaps more like a senior pastor or a presbyter in modern contexts.

Neither ministry list in I Timothy 3 exists to declare the gender of church leaders but to describe their character. Notice an overseer is required to be "blameless" (I Timothy 3:2). Many of the other descriptions are indicators of what it means to be blameless. A blameless husband is a "one-woman man." In a culture where multiple divorces and marital unfaithfulness were accepted among men, the church needed leaders devoted to one spouse. Even in polygamous cultures, women do not typically have multiple husbands.

If we were to understand "husband of one wife" to mean that only men can be pastors, then what would happen if we applied that logic to other Bible passages? Such logic might cause us to say that the Ten Commandments were only for men because they say not to covet your neighbor's wife yet say nothing about coveting someone's husband. Clearly the principle of the tenth commandment included male and female Israelites, and no believer would argue that women are free to lust after someone other than their husbands. Since the tenth commandment applied to both men and women even though the original text only refers to coveting a wife, this passage for bishops includes both genders.

Another illustration comes from passages referring to divorce. Jews would say only a husband could initiate divorce because the Hebrew Scriptures refer only to a man doing so, not a woman.[19] However, Jesus understood these passages to speak to when "a woman divorces her husband," showing us that a passage that speaks to the male gender can apply to both.[20] We are biblically correct to understand "husband of one wife" to also be applicable as "wife of one husband."

The fact that this marital statement simply describes the moral character of a pastor is evident in that a person could still be a pastor even while single like Paul or Barnabas. Jesus made it clear that marriage was not a prerequisite for ministry as it was for some official Jewish roles.[21] Paul is not saying that having a wife qualifies a man to lead a church but that such a leader must be morally faithful. A wooden way of reading I Timothy 3:2 would mean that a widowed man could not be a pastor until he remarried. It would be a mistake to misconstrue these words in a way that would disqualify Paul from the ministry!

A similar point could be made concerning children. The pastor/bishop/elder is to have "children in submission with all reverence" (I Timothy 3:4). Does this mean a man cannot be a pastor unless he has at least two children? Of course not. The principle is that the pastor be a consistent moral leader at home as well as with the church. Children do not qualify a person for ministry, but if one has children, their godly example is evidence of good leadership. We do not know if Paul had children, and Timothy probably did not either at this point. If "husband of one wife" requires that only a married man can be a pastor, then the same logic also demands that only fathers of multiple children can be pastors. However, Paul, Barnabas, and other presumably childless individuals may have been overseeing the overseers—in other words, pastoring the pastors.

Focusing too closely on the "husband of one wife" concept might demand too much from the statement. Keener says, "Paul's requirement that an overseer be 'husband of one wife' (I Timothy 3:2) is a case in point: the statement could not apply to Paul and probably could not apply to Timothy either. Does his general prohibition nullify his own teaching and that of Timothy, whom no one was to despise (4:12)?"[22] Jesus calls us to apply the broader principles of Scripture.[23] Rather than be narrow and legalistic, we have to catch the big picture. So many have strained at a gnat that they have swallowed a calling.

> *"This attribute describes the typical case of a married male leader, but the purpose is to require morality, not marriage or maleness."*
> – David K. Bernard

David Bernard says of this passage that it refers to a "person of strict sexual morality. . . . This attribute describes the typical case of a married male leader, but the purpose is to require morality, not marriage or maleness. Neither Jesus nor Paul was married, and Paul recognized female coworkers. . . . To generalize, those who are married are to be faithful to their marriage vow, and those who are single should reserve the sexual relationship for marriage."[24]

The spirit of what Paul said is: "Do not appoint a leader who has been through multiple marriages, has a live-in girlfriend, or has children that run wild." Blameless leaders are loyal and faithful to their spouses. It would be wrong to assume that since a man was not married or had no children he was a reproach. Being blameless, or above reproach, applies to a person's moral qualities and not just a specific social situation. A wise reading of Scripture catches the spirit of the teaching, not just the letter of it.

The lists for bishops and deacons are not technical lists, but general expectations. A person cannot look at one list and just go through and check them off; they are evidences of a long-term lifestyle. These qualification lists show how all believers should live. Elders are example setters. A leader needs more than a conversion story but an exemplary life to prove it. The lists in I Timothy 3 and Titus 1 reiterate what Jesus commanded: inspect a leader's fruit before we follow.[25] They give us an idea of moral blights to watch out for. We would be wise to follow these Scripture passages in examining a person's life outside the church before letting him or her influence the congregation. An honest assessment of the requirements for church leaders shows a high level of character development required for being a leader of a church.

Paul could have very simply said, "A woman cannot be a bishop." He did not say this; we cannot make his writings to say this. Paul could also have said, "A woman cannot preach or teach when men are present." He did not say this either.

We must catch the spirit behind what the Bible does say and not twist a list to prevent women from pursuing their callings.

ELDERS WHO ARE NOT OLD

The term *elder* involves both males and females. Jews would not have been surprised at a female elder. Although it appears that Jewish women living in Judea may not have had much in the way of significant leadership roles, Jewish women living outside of Palestine may have had much more influence. Archeology has revealed Jewish tombs for female elders.[26] Women also served as synagogue rulers in a variety of places.[27] A synagogue ruler kept the order and organized the events of the service.[28] Since Christianity borrowed the label of elder from the Jews, female leaders in the local congregation could have been elders.

A person was not an elder because of age necessarily but because of one's wisdom and stability. Rome appears to have been one of the key cities where women were free to lead in a variety of venues. Since the pagan religions did not allow women leaders, Christianity gave them a meaningful place to express their skills.[29] Many churches today have women whom they consider to be unofficial elders. These women pray and give solid counsel to those who ask their advice.

Peter said to the elders, "Shepherd the flock of God which is among you, serving as overseers, not by compulsion but willingly, not for dishonest gain but eagerly; nor as being lords over those entrusted to you, but being examples to the flock; and when the Chief Shepherd appears, you will receive the crown of glory that does not fade away" (I Peter 5:2–4). So, if the elders of a congregation watch for and look after others, this must be a key trait of being an elder. Can a woman look out for someone's soul? Mary and others certainly were looking out for Peter during an all-night prayer vigil.[30] In fact, such watchfulness is expected of any woman who is mature in the faith (I Timothy 5:5).

An elder must feed and shepherd the flock.[31] Can a woman feed the flock? Rachel was a shepherd of her father's flocks. Moses married a shepherd woman who had herded her father's flocks along with her sisters. If females were shepherds in that culture and time, the first hearers of this term in the church would not have thought of pastoring as a male-only activity.

What is a pastor to do? Watch out for the flock! In the church, a shepherd transfers ministerial gifts and callings,[32] handles money,[33] prays for those in need of healing,[34] and teaches.[35] They were respected above the congregation but could be reprimanded and removed if living in sin.[36] If a woman can do the work of pastoring (caring, instructing, leading, correcting), then she can be called pastor.

When Paul called together the elders of Ephesus, he told them to watch carefully for themselves and the whole flock. He told them specifically there would come men who would try to devour the congregation. Interestingly, he chose a word indicating that these threatening teachers would be males.[37] If women were a threat, one would expect such a warning about them. However, the closest we have to that is in the same letter regarding the Ephesian congregation where men are the guilty parties, leading women astray.[38]

Paul sent Titus to appoint elders in Crete.[39] He then described what such a leader should be like using the term *overseer* (bishop) in Titus 1:5–7. Then, he went on to describe male elders and female elders in Titus 2:2–5.[40] While this may be a description of older people in the church, the official designation as elder/bishop was still fluid and not a rigid office then as one might think of it today.[41] Both Paul and John's references to the church elders appear to parallel the idea of ministers in the church.[42] Furthermore, if Paul had meant to refer to old women rather than women who were elders, he could have used the same word he used in I Timothy 4:7.[43] In the context of his letter, Paul was speaking of the pastors that Titus was to appoint.[44]

The descriptions of the women elders say they are to be "teachers of good things" in Titus 2:3 which parallel the expectations of overseers to be able to teach in 1:7.[45] Female leaders have a special role in training "young women to love their husbands, to love their children" (Titus 2:4). Therefore, we cannot say a woman *can* lead in the church but that women *should* lead in the church. A male leader by himself cannot disciple the women into all they should be as wives and mothers.

JOHN'S "ELECT LADY"

It appears the apostle John wrote to a female pastor in his second epistle. Whether she was a lone leader in the local church or overseer of other pastors in that area, we do not know, but she led just the same. Was John calling a church the "elect lady" or was he speaking to a female pastor? We do not see a church referred to as a lady anywhere else. Furthermore, if "lady" refers to the church body, then who are her children he mentions?[46] It makes good sense to see this as a lady leader of a church along with those she has won to the Lord.

John calls the church members "her children" just as in other places he refers to some as "my children" (II John 1, 4, 13; III John 4). She is "elect" or "chosen"[47] and a "lady" which comes from the original word for "lord" or one with authority.[48] If this letter is to the female pastor of a flock, it is clear that John speaks to her directly ("thy" in KJV) and to all the believers ("ye" or "you"). He says to block those who do not receive the truth from "the house" (verse 10). Most likely this refers to the home where the church met together. Similarly, the writer addresses III John to a male pastor. It appears many other elect ladies pastored churches, as mentioned in the previous chapter "He Called Priscilla."

The elect lady is not alone in being a woman leader of a church, for the apostle mentions her "elect sister" also (verse

13). This cannot be referring to another church or it would be too random for the recipients of the letter to discern who the other church is. One could argue that it is a church in close proximity to the recipients' own, but if that were so, why would John need to send greetings from the church across town? Obviously he is far enough off location to have to send a letter instead of coming himself, so he certainly is not writing from a neighboring city. This probably refers to an individual. This female pastor may have had a real sister who also pastored a church and she and her congregation sent greetings through John. If he simply meant sister in the Lord, there were too many female-led congregations to narrow down which one that might be. Paul briefly mentioned multiple churches led by women, so John would not have been so vague. I believe he was speaking specifically about a congregation led by the elect lady's birth sister.

SUBMITTING AS TO ONE'S MOTHER

After describing the character expectations of an overseer, Paul also spoke about how one should behave toward these pastors. He told his protégé to treat the male pastors as fathers and the female pastors as mothers, in I Timothy 5:1–2.[49] We do not respect one over another. How does a man follow a woman pastor? Similar to how he would submit to his own dear mother.

Paul's list of requirements for pastors does not say, "Must be a good preacher, look good at conferences, and have a *Thompson-Chain Reference Bible.*" The descriptions of ministerial candidates have everything to do with their inner character, generosity, morality, and peacefulness. These are the things that make a person a natural leader. A man can graduate from seminary but still be a jerk. A person is not qualified to oversee others in the faith just because he or she knows how to study; one must grow some depth of character as well.

I watched a young man skyrocket to a place of importance because he went from being a no-name to being looked up to by everyone when he became pastor of a large church. His accomplishments preceded his character. Soon he self-destructed and took a lot of people into false doctrine with him. The biblical system of selecting the next generation of leaders works if we will value what God values, not popularity, looks, or gender. The pastor of choice will be a person who does not stir up fights, cares for others, is hospitable, stays sexually pure, and has a good reputation. Believers want to follow such a person.

Pastors are trend setters and example makers. Paul taught the young minister to "be an example to the believers in word, in conduct, in love, in spirit, in faith, in purity" and to be "showing yourself to be a pattern of good works" (I Timothy 4:12; Titus 2:7). Jesus showed us how the shepherd should live in humble service as a role model.[50] Can a godly woman set an example for others to follow? Can she live a life of sacrifice, humility, and service to others? Then, yes, she can also do the work of a pastor, if God so called her.

Many pastors' wives do pastoral ministry, but without the title of pastor. My wife is the personable side of our ministry. People love her for her spirit and ability to easily connect with others. I am the bookish, systematized person who struggles to be a conversationalist. Though my wife has no plans to get up and speak in church, I might not have a crowd to speak to if it were not for her balance in my ministry. She is the one who does well at one-on-one ministry and counseling—which is as much the work of a pastor as pulpit ministry.

A title of pastor, elder, or bishop signifies a person's commitment to doing the work of ministry. Unfortunately, many are still reticent to give the same title to a woman that they give to a man in the same position. For example, a woman who leads the youth will often be called a "youth leader" but a man gets the title "youth pastor" or "student pastor." Or a man leading the children might be called "children's pastor" but a woman in the same position might be called "children's ministry director."[51]

The question is not so much deciding on whom *we* will call pastor, but of whom *God* will call pastor. We are not the ones who bestow these callings. The Lord calls; we just repeat after Him. The church must recognize those He has called.

The question is not so much deciding on whom we will call pastor, but of whom God will call pastor.

Of course, we should not make a big deal out of labels anyway. Jesus warned about pompous leaders:

> They love . . . to be called by men, 'Rabbi, Rabbi.' But you, do not be called 'Rabbi'; for One is your Teacher, the Christ, and you are all brethren. Do not call anyone on earth your father; for One is your Father, He who is in heaven. And do not be called teachers; for One is your Teacher, the Christ. But he who is greatest among you shall be your servant. And whoever exalts himself will be humbled, and he who humbles himself will be exalted.[52]

Any label can become a pride thing. God's people should not be label-hungry, but service oriented. More important than the title before your name is what comes after it. What kinds of people follow you? Who are you leading and how are they becoming like Jesus? Minister is a calling; teaching is a gift; prophet is a ministry; bishop is a good work; pastor is a weighty responsibility.

There are no biblical restrictions preventing a woman from serving others. No commands against her casting out demons, speaking faith, healing the ill, or baptizing a convert. Since no barriers exist to prevent a woman from doing the work of the ministry, we cannot rightly bar her from pastoral ministry. Like Paul, may we inspire many leaders in the church.

Paul had been barred from continuing his ministry pursuit in a certain region. God slammed the doors in his face and gave him a vision. Then, the winds of change moved the ship at full sail, straight toward his next ministry venture. God knew there was a Lydia waiting to be the first European and the first westerner to accept the gospel message. Paul brought the gospel from the East and found the home of a woman to be the first base he could work out of to present the plan of salvation. May we in the West be just as receptive of God's calling on women as that woman was of God's calling on a man.

10 | He Called Eve: Women as Ladies

Must women be submitted to men to do ministry?

> *And the LORD God caused a deep sleep to fall on Adam, and he slept; and He took one of his ribs, and closed up the flesh in its place. Then the rib which the LORD God had taken from man He made into a woman, and He brought her to the man. And Adam said: "This is now bone of my bones And flesh of my flesh; She shall be called Woman, Because she was taken out of Man" (Genesis 2:21–23).*

Adam saw no flaw in the woman God had made for him. There in a well-landscaped park, he and his wife shared a role as rulers of the planet. When the Lord first made them, He told them to subdue the earth and have dominion (Genesis 1:28). The Lord gave the first leadership position to a male and a female, they were to subdue and have dominion together.[1] This was how things worked before sin. He made man and woman *both* in His image.

Some would claim that God gave shared leadership to men and women because they are equal. I disagree. He included both in leadership because they are different. Men and women have different perspectives on many things and the Lord saw the importance of unity in that diversity.

T. W. Barnes said,

> I think every preacher needs input from great women. I like to hear how they think. In 1913, the year I was born, Mary Woodworth Etter hit the sawdust trail across America with a ministry of signs, wonders, miracles and a mighty outpouring of the Holy Ghost. In the early days of Pentecost, God not only raised up mighty men, but He raised up mighty women to preach the Gospel. Aimee Semple McPherson and others drew great crowds and many people received healing and the Holy Ghost.[2]

We need the diversity women in ministry can bring today.

Not everyone sees women as a blessing. To the Jews, Eve was the cause of sin and women had to pay for what she had done. Some Reformed scholars have also argued that Eve proved that her gender is not fit to lead because she gave in to the tempter. They say that since "the serpent took the initiative to tempt Eve rather than Adam," this proves she took part in "subverting the pattern of male leadership."[3] However, in Genesis 3:6, Adam was "with her" during this temptation and was just as responsible. Paul did not indicate that the woman was to blame for sin, but pointed the finger at Adam, explaining that "through one man sin entered the world."[4] A believer should not treat women as if they are more easily deceived, nor do we blame them for sin any more than we should blame men for weeds and thorns.

Eve was not created as a subset of humanity or a different species from Adam. She was made from him to balance the human race. Before she came along, God looked at lonely Adam and said, "It is not good that man should be alone." After presenting Eve as the finishing touch to His creation, He looked at everything He had made and said things were very good.[5] Now, we will look at how Paul used the story of the first man and woman to illustrate a spiritual truth in I Corinthians 11.

WHO IS IN CHARGE HERE?

Consider the typical perception of this phrase: "the head of every man is Christ, the head of woman is man, and the head of Christ is God" (11:3). At first glance, this might appear to a Western mind to say the man is in charge of the woman. However, does this mean that Christ is in charge of only the man? If we followed such logic, the woman would have to approach Christ only through a man! Certain branches of Christianity believe a male religious leader (a priest) has to be the people's connection to God, but Pentecostals reject such notions. Therefore, it would be a theological clash to say a man stands between the woman and Christ.

A proper understanding of the word head in this passage will prevent much misunderstanding in the discussion regarding the role of women. In western culture, we use the phrase "is the head of" to describe someone who is in charge of something. Eastern thinking is not so limited in this expression. Even in our own vocabulary, the word "head" can be used in a variety of ways.[6] We might say things "came to a head" indicating some conflict, keep a "cool head" meaning to handle stress well, or that one should "get his head together" indicating thinking things through. Such a variety of meanings existed in ancient usage as well. Head could refer to authority, but it also could mean source or beginning. For example, the "head of the river" meant the point of the river's beginning. Rosh Hashanah, the Hebrew phrase for New Year, simply means "head of the year." No one would take such phrases to mean the head of the river controls what the river does or that the first day of the year takes authority over the other days of the year. The simple understanding is that head in these statements means "point of beginning." Adam was the head, the point of beginning, of Eve. This makes best sense of the rest of the passage in I Corinthians 11.

Unfortunately, some use this passage to define a chain of command. The umbrella explanation goes like this: God is over Christ, Christ is over man, man is over woman. If a woman wants the blessings of God, she has to be under a man. Such an explanation goes so far as to say that if she steps out from under a man, "her covering," then she steps out from under Christ and God. The practical conclusion some make from such a teaching is that a woman needs a man present if she is going to preach or teach. If this is true, a woman cannot teach a children's class or even a home Bible study without a man present. Using such logic, someone said a ladies' conference needs a man in the room so the women are not without a covering. However, the biblical covering for a woman is her hair (11:15), not a man. The passage says nothing about an umbrella, a *man covering*, or a chain of command. In fact, Paul makes a statement later to guard against such an interpretation, as we will examine.

This mistaken view comes in part because of a mental rewriting of the passage. It does not say God > Christ > man > woman. Instead of a flow of command, the text presents the flow of the Creation sequence. A proper flow chart of how Paul wrote this would look more like:

Christ → man → woman
God → Christ

Christ is the point of beginning of the man.[7] Man was created in the image of God (Genesis 1:27) and we know that the foreordained image of God is the man Jesus Christ (John 1:1–2, 14; Colossians 1:15). Therefore, the planned Christ was the pattern or source for man.[8] Then, in turn, Adam was the point of beginning for Eve, being that the Lord created her from his side. And then, the next creative work took place many thousands of years later as Christ came into existence, His point of beginning being God.

Paul stated things in the historical order of how creation occurred. This order prepares the reader for what he will say next about glory. Who you are and what you do reflects glory somewhere other than yourself:

God's glory is a godly man.
A man's glory is a godly woman.[9]
Finally, a woman's glory is her uncut hair.[10]

Glory also means splendor, brightness, and by implication, beauty. Jesus Christ shows the brightness and beauty of our God.[11] The role of humans is to enhance the splendor and glory of the Lord. Women beautify the human race (sorry, men, I know you try hard to look good, but the women have us beat). A woman's uncut hair is her glory and beauty.

In the rural area where my wife and I have raised our children, an acquaintance made big money in the trash removal industry. Bobby went door-to-door many years ago and got customers signed up on his trash collection service and bought a garbage truck. After a short time of making a decent income hauling trash, he accepted an offer from the competing company from whom he took many customers. They paid him one million dollars for his little business. If you heard Bobby brag about trash trucking, you can be sure the glory is not in the product but in the profit he hauled from that venture.

The glory of the garbage industry is in the cash, not the trash. Who would want to go around just collecting garbage for no purpose? There has to be something more glorious to make it meaningful. Likewise, our glory is not in ourselves. A man who devalues women is like a garbage truck driver who works for free—worthless and stinky.

START AT THE BEGINNING

If Paul intended to present males as dominant over females, he could have said the man was lord over the woman.[12] However, Jesus instructed us not to be lords over one another. Therefore, to make this passage about men having hierarchical control over women would defy Jesus' own teaching. If we are talking about a flow of authority from God down to women, it would seem ridiculous to the Pentecostal mind to think that if a woman were to give a message of prophecy that she would have to get clearance with a male superior before doing so. When we understand this passage as being a discussion about created order, it is no longer in conflict with the rest of the Scriptures, including the very next chapter in I Corinthians on spiritual gifts!

This translation of head as a source or a point of beginning appears to be in keeping with Paul's use of the term elsewhere. In another place, Paul referred to Christ as "the head" of the church and described our connection as, "the body, nourished and knit together by joints and ligaments" (Colossians 2:19). We flow out of Him, our point of beginning and spiritual life source. Paul also wrote that we "may grow up in all things into Him who is the head—Christ—from whom the whole body, joined and knit together by what every joint supplies" (Ephesians 4:15–16). Clearly, we have a Source and our lives reflect that connection.

To prevent any misconceptions in his use of the term head, Paul returned to this thought in I Corinthians 11:8. Woman must be distinct from man because "man is not from woman, but woman from man." This restates the idea of the order of creation: she came from him. If anything, this is a good case against feminism. A woman is not equal to a man, but must retain her distinctiveness. "Neither," verse 11 says, "is man independent of woman, nor woman independent of man, in the Lord." In verse 12, Paul put in his disclaimer so no one would think this was about men being superior to or in authority over women: "For as woman came from man, even so man also comes through woman; but all things are from God." Neither is better, but both are unique.

A catch phrase among some Christians is "heads of the church," or "department heads." These phrases assume that certain individuals are heads of the church. Combining this idea with the misunderstanding of I Corinthians 11, one could incorrectly assume that if men are the heads, then church heads must be male. However, church leaders are not called heads in the Scriptures.

There is only one head in a body. He who called the apostles, prophets, evangelists, pastors, and teachers is Himself "the head—Christ"! We are all knit together as a body with one another, connected to our one source, Jesus, the Head of the church (Ephesians 4:11–16). Spiritually speaking, there are not males and females in the body of Christ for all are one in Him. Gender and racial barriers melt away, says Galatians 3:28: "There is neither Jew nor Greek, there is neither slave nor free, there is neither male nor female; for you are all one in Christ Jesus."[13]

> *We are all knit together as a body with one another, connected to our one source, Jesus, the Head of the church.*

HER GOD-GIVEN COVERING

Evangelicals often argue that Pentecostals have gotten their understanding of hair wrong. Most holiness Pentecostals would declare the importance of women keeping their hair long, but we have not been so consistent in our defense of women in ministry. While the teaching of long hair on women is important, a person's identity and perhaps eternal destiny is also tied to his or her calling. We cannot put women in ministry if it is wrong, but we cannot deny them from their proper role if this is what God desires. I was once guilty of being well-aware of one scriptural truth (gender distinction in hair) while neglecting another one of great weight (women in full ministry capacities).

A popular family seminar series in the past few decades has spread a belief that women are incomplete without men.[14] A marginal note provided by translators in an early English Bible version fueled such thinking centuries ago. Where the KJV of I Corinthians 11:10 says, the woman ought to have "power on her head," a footnote explained the woman's covering this way: "That is, a covering in sign that she is under the power of her husband." This turns the verse upside down, saying she is the one yielding power instead of the one wielding power.[15] Thus, male commentators repurposed the woman's passage to mean that a woman needs a man for a covering. This seems to be reversed from the simple creation story. Woman was given to complete the man, not the man to complete the woman.

Can a woman hear from God directly or does she need a man who mediates for her? One woman listened to the voice of God for herself:

> David Heath agonized as his eldest daughter told him of her burden for Japan. "Oh, May, I cannot bear to give you up. Our family would be too lonely and bereft. You know we have already lost two of our dear children. Baby Mabel, and then three weeks later, before we could even reach him, our Walter died in college. Please don't go."
>
> "But, Papa, God is calling me, and I have so wanted to work for Him."
>
> "Dear May, surely you can find a work to do for the Lord in this country; besides, I have never even seen a Japanese. What kind of people are they? Are they barbarians or cannibals?"
>
> "Dear, dear Papa, I must go. The burden for Japan is great. They worship many, many ugly gods of fear, and the great masses have never even heard the name of Jesus. I hear them calling me night and day. Though I love you dearly and it almost breaks my heart to leave all my family, the call of God is strong. I must go."
>
> It was 1902, May Heath, a single lady, at age twenty-five, was going to far-off Japan, the field of labor she felt the Lord had put on her heart. She had always been hungry for the Lord and had a deep desire to serve Him.[16]

While a young woman under her parents' care needs to respect their wishes, God will call her directly one day. Just as Jesus submitted Himself until His ministry moment came, we all live to do the will of the Father. In the Esther chapter, we applaud the biblical principle of submission to authority; however, we cannot substitute that doctrine with the idea of submission to men.

To those who claim a woman must hear from God through a man, I must point out:

- Gabriel spoke to young Mary first (not her father) before informing her fiancé.
- The Angel of the Lord appeared to Samson's mom first and then his dad second.
- Ruth got a legal resolution to her dilemma because she courageously addressed the situation. The men involved only got involved because she did.
- Lydia hosted a women's prayer meeting in Philippi (Acts 16:13). Even though they had no "male covering," God answered their prayers by sending them the gospel.

The theory of males being the covering falls short of biblical support.

Another anti-women-in-ministry explanation for I Corinthians 11 incorrectly explains: "When women pray and prophesy, they must adorn themselves properly, thereby indicating they are supportive of male leadership in the church."[17] Instead, this passage means a woman operating in spiritual authority must live in recognition of who created her. She does need to walk in submission to her husband, if married, but not to males in general—an impossibility. Many believed because of the testimony of the woman at the well. What male authority was this divorced woman under since she had no husband? Her authority was Jesus Himself—the same authority every minister must have.

As we saw with I Timothy 2:11–12, confusion arises when someone takes a Scripture passage about husbands and wives and applies it to women in ministry. Look closely at the text where some of this discussion arises:

> Every man praying or prophesying, having his head covered, dishonors his head. But every woman who prays or prophesies with her head uncovered *dishonors her head*, for that is one and the same as if her head were shaved. For if a woman is not covered, let her also be shorn. But if it is shameful for a woman to be shorn or shaved, *let her be covered*. For a man indeed ought not to cover his head, since he is the image and glory of God; but woman is the glory of man.... But if a woman has long hair, it is a glory to her; for *her hair is given to her for a covering* (I Corinthians 11:4–7, 15, emphasis added).

Jewish traditions prevented a woman from speaking in an assembly, but Paul says a woman should pray and prophesy! Physical distinctions must be maintained between both men and women, but both can serve out loud. This passage does not say women *may* speak in the meeting, but indicates that they *should*. Such teaching was countercultural for Jewish women and even many Greeks.[18] Every believer should pray and every believer should desire to prophesy. More than just informing women of their opportunity to join in the worship service, this passage lets them know how to serve in the Spirit with proper authority and decorum.

> *This passage does not say women may speak in the meeting, but indicates that they should.*

A HAIR SHORT OF GLORY

Neither Paul nor the first readers of this letter thought of this passage to be about whether a woman could be a pastor or not. It speaks about how she is to walk in spiritual power:

"For this reason the woman ought to have. . . authority on her head, because of the angels."[19] While verse 10 perplexes many with what it might mean, it shows that this dialogue hinges on spiritual authority, not hierarchical or institutional authority. In contrast to those who use I Corinthians 11 to say authority does not belong to the woman, the center of this passage plainly says she has authority.

Jesus never used this word *authority* in reference to His followers leading or commanding one another. He spoke of authority as being what the church has over demons and the work of the enemy. A Spirit-filled woman does not need a man to rebuke a demon for her, she can do that herself. Jesus did not require that a male be present for His church to have spiritual authority. We need to submit ourselves to church leadership not because of their gender, but because of their calling and faithfulness to the message of Truth they proclaim.

Angels, agents of God's power, are watching those who celebrate their gender distinction.[20] Those who rebel against their God ordained place (as did Lucifer) incur disfavor from heaven. In a world where gender confusion abounds, the woman should not blur her female distinction if she wants to walk in the favor of God. As I Corinthians points out, her head covering is her uncut hair, a living witness that she embraces whom God made her to be.

Some have used I Corinthians to say a woman should wear a head cloth or veil on her head. Instead, the passage does not say for a woman to wear a covering, but that it was her hair the Lord had "given to her for a covering." The word veil does not even enter this discussion, even though Jewish women were accustomed to wearing a cloth head covering.

There could not have been a custom in "all the churches" for women to wear veils because elsewhere, Paul had to teach against the weaving of gold and jewels into the women's hairdos. If their hair had been under veils, no one would have seen the jewelry in it. Surely if this passage were about a woman wearing a head-covering so she could pray or prophesy, then would God not hear a man today who prayed while wearing his winter hat or a hoodie?

This passage clearly teaches the importance of maintaining visual distinctions in gender. A man must cut his hair because hair hanging down is a dishonor for him (verse 14). A woman reflects the glory of God by growing out her hair. She grows it out, in contrast to the man who cuts his. While other Pentecostal writings deal more thoroughly with this topic, it is important to note that cutting bangs or trimming her hair would defy the order to grow it out.

God created Adam and shortly afterward had to cut on him. He had to have surgery so Eve could be made. But the woman was the final piece of all creation, and God did not cut on her afterward. God made His bride complete in Him; she is pure and perfect because of Him. Christ had to be cut on with a whip and with a spear in his side. Out of that side came His bride, the blood and water being what sanctifies the church. Perhaps gender distinctions in hair can help us remember our place in creation and in reflecting the eternal story of Christ and His church.

The man is the glory of God, the "woman is the glory of man" (I Corinthians 11:7), and the glory of the woman is her hair (11:15). Just as Scripture plainly states that a woman should not cut on her glory, her hair, so the man should not *cut* on his glory, the woman. Husbands who denigrate or subjugate their wives are trimming back their own glory. Rather than curtail a woman's service to the Lord, a man should encourage her to grow to her full potential.

FEMININITY, NOT FEMINISM

In addition to feminine hair, a woman also maintains her gender distinction by modesty of dress and her way of presenting herself. T. W. Barnes said that the Lord

> will use a woman if she remains feminine. I have watched some great lady preachers get derailed because they became masculine. The ladies turn off an effeminate preacher. If a woman is masculine, the men turn her off. The Lord will bless a lady preacher who stays feminine; He releases His message through her, as through a man, but He uses her different approach and outlook to enhance the ministry.[21]

Nothing about preaching or ministering is masculine only. A woman does not need to growl or stomp like some men do in order to get across a powerful sermon. (I would imagine most men do not need to resort to such behavior either.) We should all seek to be what Christ desires us to be and not conform to the image of anyone else. Whether she is parenting, preaching, praying, or prophesying, a woman's uncut hair and other feminine distinctives in her clothing keep her from being just one of the guys.[22] Paul worked to guard against those who would masculinize the women or feminize the men.[23]

> *"The Lord will bless a lady preacher who stays feminine."*
> *— T. W. Barnes*

We live in a gender-confused world and the church needs to help clarify gender roles, not blur them. Unfortunately, many church groups have blurred gender roles in the way they dress. Gender distinction prevents gender confusion. American women started wearing pants back in the aftermath of the women's lib campaigns when they took over men's jobs in the WWII era. Yves Saint Laurent was instrumental in taking French lesbian fashions from the 1920s and 30s and incorporating them into the "sexy but not girlie" pantsuit called Le Smoking. While many would argue that women's pants are not the same as men's pants, it is interesting that a cross-dressing man usually chooses a skirt to imitate a woman, not pants.

I am thankful for the position the United Pentecostal Church has taken for generations. We have consistently taught our women to be ladies by letting their hair grow and our men to look like the males God created them to be by cutting it short. We have consistently taught our women to look distinct from men by wearing flowing dresses and skirts that do not draw attention to anatomy but state boldly their gender.

I would say the example set by the male ministers in our movement has been distinctly masculine for many years. By staying strong regarding gender distinctives, the trends in the music industry and society in general will not work into our ranks and try to effeminize our young men or masculinize our girls. Today's youth are the next generation's leaders.

WOMAN AS THE HELPER

God called Eve Adam's helper, a suitable companion that complemented his body and his purpose. Both were made to meet each other's needs and to work in unity toward the mission. God did not form Eve so Adam would have someone to make the eggs and toast while he went about the important things in life. He created her to join him in the important things in life.

The most common use of this word translated "helper" in Scripture refers to God helping His people.[24] This term does not indicate one who is below the other, for God is certainly not less than His people. It is a term of teamwork, of partnering together. In the New Testament, the Spirit is our "Helper."

Since Calvinists who oppose women speaking in the church also oppose speaking in tongues, both types of helper are undervalued in their belief system. Those in the Pentecostal experience find the stakes higher. What would our movement be if the Spirit no longer helped in our services? We need our Helper from above and men need to recognize that their complementary creation, women, must help in the ministry as well.

A common social stereotype is that men and women are in conflict. God did not create a problem between sexes; He created a unity and joint purpose. If there is an imbalance between men and women, it exists for the same reason as historical tension between races: because of sin.

When the spirit of teamwork catches on, men not only give women a space but even give up their own spaces. This would be similar to the dynamics of finding a child in need. You could tell others they need to feed him or you could give up the burger you were about to eat. To have women in leadership is to trust them with decision making, not having them raise funds only to tell them how to spend it. This means ordaining women, inviting them to speak at our camp meetings, and supporting them in making decisions alongside men in crucial matters.

11 | He Called Ruth: Women as Wives

Is a wife subjected to her husband?

Who can find a virtuous wife? For her worth is far above rubies. The heart of her husband safely trusts her; so he will have no lack of gain. She does him good and not evil all the days of her life (Proverbs 31:10–12).

I have found a treasure in my Leanne, whom I am always careful to not refer to as just "the wife." My hard-working, adventure-loving, and resourceful wife is a talented musician, educating parent, and loyal spouse. Money cannot measure the extreme value my bride has added to my life. Another man felt that way about a girl from Moab who stands as a role model of godly behavior for all young women.

Ruth could have followed the bad advice of her bitter mother-in-law to go back to the gods of the heathens around her but she wanted to know the One True God. She wanted to be associated with the people of God and not blend with the world. Hard-working, full of faith, kind to the elderly, respectful of the dead, hungry for the things of God, and full of hope, Ruth received an accolade no other woman in Scripture is recorded as having. Boaz praised her, saying, "All the people of my town know that you are a virtuous woman"

(Ruth 3:11). This woman, who did not grow up in a godly environment and was trying to survive as a widow without social power or financial resources, got the high praise every Hebrew wife might wish for, "You are a virtuous woman!"

A woman with a history against her (her Moabite ancestry), and a failed marriage (her husband died leaving her no son—a social disgrace in that day) became an exemplary woman in Israel. Not only did she become grandmother to King David but she also took part in the genealogy of Jesus Christ.[1] The book of wise sayings highlights the importance of finding a woman of high moral character. Using the exact words as came from Boaz's lips, Proverbs 31:10 asks, "Who can find a virtuous woman?" In some versions of the Hebrew Bible, Ruth follows Proverbs directly as the answer to that question.[2] Perhaps having his great-great-grandmother in mind, Solomon's book of wisdom tells other young men to find a wife like Ruth.

More than just a role model for young women today, Ruth's selfless surrender to be the wife of Boaz is a picture of how the church, the bride of Christ, should submit itself to the Lord.[3] As Boaz was the man willing to redeem Ruth and take her under his protective care, so Christ reaches out in love to His bride and lavishes us with His attention. God gave the husband and wife relationship to preach the message of Christ and the church (not as a pattern for ministry in the church).[4]

For those who are unmarried, this chapter may not hold immediate personal benefit. However, I have included it mainly because I have discovered that a dim view of women in ministry is often paired with a low view of women in general. This particularly manifests in the way men treat their wives and how wives view themselves as well.

Part of my clarity on women in ministry came when I got a right understanding of the woman in my home. Somehow I read too much into the command for a wife to submit. I did not understand what it meant to cherish one's wife. Perhaps this chapter can help some other man like the over-demanding, young husband I used to be.

COUNTER-PARTNERS

Throughout this book, I have not used the phrase *opposite sex*. God did not make men and women to be opposed. He created a husband and wife to be one. Opposition in marriage is from sin and leads to death of the relationship.

God did not look at Adam and say, "I need to create him an opposite. The poor man has nothing to oppose him." No, He created the man a suitable counterpart, a complementary partner. One writer has called her the counterpartner.[5] She filled in where he was lacking and he fills in where she is lacking. She provides him emotional support, perhaps children, and a sense of completeness. He provides her security, life necessities, and leadership.

These roles work in a marriage. They fall apart when we try to apply them to men and women in general or the church as a whole. Women are not my counterpartners; only my wife is. Women are not complementary to men; a wife is complementary to her husband (they should both be complimentary toward one another as well!). The problem with many who are against women in ministry is that they try to take what the Bible says about wives and apply it to women in general.

> *Too many make the mistake of taking what the Bible says about wives and applying it to women in general.*

Complementarity is like a fork and a spoon. Neither one does exactly the same job. Neither is better than the other. They both have different purposes. Where the wife nurtures and takes care of immediate needs, the husband leads, protects, and takes care of the larger needs of the family. God put a man and woman together as a team.

There is little equality between men and women. This is not to suggest any inferiority. Those who say men and women should be equal might mistakenly believe inequality means inferiority. To say the fork is not equal with the spoon is not to say the fork is inferior to the spoon. With lamb roast, I want a fork; with cream of broccoli soup, I want a spoon. Both tools are useful in their proper setting. This being said, such inequality pertains to the home and family relationships, not essentially to the church.

To say the church does not have complementarity between the sexes means that there is no spiritual role a woman cannot do. She can work miracles, preach, cast out demons, pastor, and teach as well as a man can because we have the same Spirit of God. This is where Calvinists who oppose women in ministry mistake the complementarity between husband and wife as applying to men and women generally.

For example, just as it is wrong to apply Bible passages regarding husbands and wives to all men and women, it would also be wrong to take Scripture verses speaking to masters and slaves as applying to all rich and poor people. Though my neighbor's net worth is ten times my own, I do not have to submit to his leadership. We are equal as citizens. If he was my boss, however, I would submit to his leadership; and if I were his boss, he would have to obey me, no matter how rich he was. Similarly, just because my wife follows my leadership does not mean she should follow the leadership of all men or all husbands.

ROLE-MODEL MARRIAGE

The husband and wife paint a picture of Christ and the church, His Bride. Spiritually, the complementarity is not between men and women but between the church as a whole and Jesus Christ. The church is the counterpartner to Christ. We are the spiritual birthers, nurses, and nurturers while He protects us and provides all that we need for spiritual life. We, whom He has called His Bride, follow His leadership and guidance in all things.

The husband has the biggest challenge in the marriage. The part Paul addressed to husbands does not tell him he is the head. I have heard many men say, "I am the head of the house." The Bible does not say, "Man, you are the head of that woman, so take charge." Scripture calls the husband to something much more substantial than that.

Let's look at what Ephesians 5:25–33 tells the guys:

> Husbands, love your wives, just as Christ also loved the church and *gave Himself* for her, that He might *sanctify and cleanse her* with the washing of water by the word, that He might *present her to Himself* a glorious church, not having spot or wrinkle or any such thing, but that she should be holy and without blemish. So husbands *ought to love their own wives* as their own bodies; he who loves his wife loves himself. For no one ever hated his own flesh, but nourishes and cherishes it, just as the Lord does the church. For we are members of His body, of His flesh and of His bones. "For this reason a man shall leave his father and mother and be joined to his wife, and the two shall become one flesh." This is a great mystery, but I speak concerning Christ and the church. Nevertheless let each one of you in particular so *love his own wife as himself*, and let the wife see that she respects her husband. (Emphasis added.)

I struggle to grasp the magnitude of what it means that I, as a husband, am to give myself for my wife. In most cultures, women serve the men. In the biblical model, however, the husband gives himself for the wife.

A husband must wash his wife with his words like Christ does the church. Just as a woman is not to cut the glory off her head, the husband is not to cut down his glory, his wife. It would be too easy for me to chop at my wife with complaints or criticism. She does not need me to do surgery on her, however. I must beautify her with my words. A husband needs to also take time to discuss the Scriptures and wash his wife with God's Word as well. Although this topic deserves its own book, I address some of this here to lay out a wide-angle view on the topic of women in ministry.

THE HUSBAND GIVES HIMSELF

Christ "gave Himself" for His Bride. Such total dedication and self-sacrifice seems out of reach, yet He calls me to duplicate Him in my marriage. I can only do that by being led by His Spirit. The simple key to a strong marriage is to follow the golden rule. If husbands would treat their wives the way they want to be treated, most marriage counselors would be unemployed. Of course what a man wants from the relationship may not be what she wants or needs from the relationship. The bigger principle, then, is to make his wife feel the way he would want to feel: loved, needed, safe, cherished.

A husband must do nothing "through selfish ambition or conceit, but in lowliness of mind" should esteem his wife "better than himself." He must "look out not only for his own interests, but also for the interests of" his spouse. Where do we learn this? "Let this mind be in you which was also in Christ Jesus," who "made Himself of no reputation, taking the form of a bondservant," and gave the ultimate gift of Himself (Philippians 2:3–7). This is nothing more than the life all Christians are called to.

A husband loves his wife as his own body. Eve came from Adam's rib; by faith, a wife today is from her husband's side—bone of his bone and flesh of his flesh. Even the church came from the Second Adam's side where the blood and water flowed. No sane person destroys his own body but helps it stay healthy and productive. No wise husband destroys his body: his wife. Making her look good makes him look good.

A healthy marriage is a couple who are enjoying life together. You look at them and you could not tell who is in charge. They work in harmony. She has joyfully chosen to trust His leadership, and he has sacrificially chosen to lead in her best interest.

THE HEAD OF THE HOME

A church in right relationship with her Husband shows the joy of the Lord. A brow-beaten, crippled church is a body of believers who have not discovered the joy of submission. They fuss and kick against His leadership, wanting to do their own thing. Hence, there are "wars and fights" among them arising from the believers' "desires for pleasure."[6] No wonder such a body of believers would be called "Adulterers and adulteresses!"[7] God wants a loyal spouse just as one would expect in a healthy marriage.

The way husbands treat their wives and wives treat their husbands preaches a message concerning Christ and the church. I must be Christ to her; she must be to me what the church is to Christ. Every couple should earnestly work toward this art of living. I must say, my wife has her role down much better than I.

Here is what the book of Ephesians says to the married woman:

> "Wives, submit to your own husbands, as to the Lord. For the husband is head of the wife, as also Christ is head of the church; and He is the Savior of the body. Therefore, just as the church is subject to Christ, so let the wives be to their own husbands in everything" (5:22–24).[8]

The verse just before this passage says, we are to be "submitting to one another in the fear of God." Wives submit to their husbands with respect and honor. Husbands submit to their wives with love and nurturing care.

A wife submits to her husband because he is her head the way Christ is head of the church. Jesus became head of the church by being "Savior of the body." Christ's self-sacrifice began the church. So, Christ is the head in the sense of beginning the church. We, the church, submit to Christ because without Him we would not exist.

This message from Paul to husbands and wives concludes in verse 33 with "let the wife see that she respects her husband." Peter said she should respect him "as Sarah obeyed Abraham, calling him lord,"[9] or calling him "sir." He is her Adam, by faith, and she looks to him as her source of origin.

Many women have never had a role model to follow in how to submit. Fortunately, submission is not a thing just for wives, but every believer is called to submit. In I Corinthians 16:16 and I Peter 5:5, the same word is used for everyone in the church as the word used for wives in Ephesians 5:22. Every godly man must submit, too. If a woman married to a believer wants to know how to submit, she needs merely follow the example of how her husband submits to his pastor.

> *If a woman married to a believer wants to know how to submit, she needs merely follow the example of how her husband submits to his pastor.*

CONNECTING HEAD AND BODY

Too many marriages these days are headless, in the sense that the husband (head) is absent most of the time. I remember being the man who would be gone from home most of the week and only come home each day long enough to complain about how the kids were doing things. Instead of actually being the source of life to the family, I was a drain on it. While we let women find their purpose in the Kingdom, many of us married men need to pursue a better understanding of our calling to headship in the home, to being the life-source for our families.

When our third daughter was three months old she contracted botulism. First she began to lose the ability to suck and would hardly eat. Over a few days she slowly lost muscle control. When we picked her up and her head flopped backward, we knew she had to have medical help. At the closest emergency room we could get her to, she coded blue. She did not have the strength to breathe on her own. After a helicopter flight to St. Louis Children's Hospital, we found experts who knew what to do.

One specialist walked up to me and said, "Hi, I'm Dr. Smith with infectious diseases."[10] I did not want to shake the hand of anyone who might be contagious, but I figured out what she meant rather quickly. This doctor taught us a lot. She said botulism starts in the head (droopy eyelids, loss of ability to swallow) and works from the core outward through the rest of the body. Eventually the whole body becomes paralyzed—as our daughter's was at that moment. Thank God for the people who were praying for her at the camp meeting in St. Louis (which we had to leave for this emergency). We felt those prayers and saw her condition improve even before the medicine (valued in six digits) had arrived.

Like botulism, problems in the home often start with the head as well. How would Christian marriages be different if our men realized they were the point of beginning for the home? If the home lacks joy and harmony, the man needs to take a look at himself. If the marriage is full of fighting and selfishness, troubleshooting begins with the head. Realizing this has made me work harder on me than on my wife or kids. If there is something in our family I do not like, it often indicates that I have to make some changes myself.

The head does what is best for the body; it does not try to destroy it. If you knew someone who kept cutting himself, you might say he was out of his head. If a man verbally cuts down his wife or jabs at her with his words, he is out of his head, Jesus Christ. If a wife cuts down her man, she is out of her head, the husband. An adulterous wife is beheading herself.[11]

If we want the favor of the Lord, we must get our "head" on straight. Jesus, our Head, is where everything begins. We demonstrate our theological understanding of this truth by how husbands and wives treat one another. Unity in marriage will model the Christ/Bride relationship correctly. If we lose our heads, the body will be paralyzed. By being the husbands and wives Scripture teaches us to be, we can see a sustainable move of God.

In the first-century world, women had to obey their husbands for fear of violence. This passage in Ephesians teaches them to make the choice to submit, not because they had to but because they were doing it unto the Lord. Women in that day were treated as inferior to men in every way and could only express their opinions in their own home.[12] Some male dominance arose likely because men were typically old enough to be the fathers of the wives they chose. Since she knew little to nothing, she was safest to do whatever he said and he gladly accepted the opportunity to be an overlord.[13] God's Word, however, restructures the marriage around the idea of love and care for each other.

Two things will happen when we get a biblical understanding of the husband/wife relationship: marriages will never be the same and the church will never be the same. When a wife and husband team up in submission and cherishing, one can hardly tell who the boss of the relationship is. A loving husband giving himself for his wife does not look like a commando driving her every move. He looks more like the butler with the towel on his arm. A woman in such a marriage will be far more liberated than all the obstinate "I did it my way" attempts at independence the world has lured her with.

He and she are one flesh in marriage. It has been this way since God made Eve from Adam's side. When a man marries a woman, he is to take by faith that this is the woman God made for him. Adam had no one else to turn to for marriage in that Garden. You are in the Garden of God and have no other spouse available. In Christ, you are one flesh with the person to whom you are married.

Every married woman has a ministry in tandem with her husband's calling. Many men are tempted to chase their own ministries, leaving the wife behind. God created Eve as a counterpartner to join her husband in his calling. Husbands would do so much for healing the role of women in the church by including them in their own ministries.

HOW TO ENJOY LIFE

Husband, love your wife as your own self. Paul spoke to the men in Ephesus telling them not to be angry, doubtful, and disputing, but to be men of prayer. Apostle Peter also said as much to the husbands: "dwell with them with understanding, giving honor to the wife, as to the weaker vessel, and as *being heirs together* of the grace of life, that your *prayers may not be hindered.*"[14] The chapter on Eve pointed out that the way a woman treats her glory (her hair) affects angelic involvement. Here we learn that the way a husband treats his glory (his wife) affects his interactions with heaven, too: "that your prayers may not be hindered."

Abraham thought the blessing was all about him. It seemed he had a hard time getting the idea that the promised descendants would come through Sarah. He tried to have a baby with another woman and created a mess for everyone. Finally, he understood that the promise would come through him *and* his wife. Here she was, faithful and loyal, setting an example of meekness for women of faith today, and there he went, plowing through life trying to find his purpose without her. Fortunately he got it right by age 99!

Husbands, we must dwell with our wives in an understanding way. Just as we want our wives to honor us, we must honor them. We handle them as if they were an expensive vase, as if they were weaker vessels. This is not to say they are weaker. A woman must be tough to birth children. Not many men have nerves enough to fix a meal, change a diaper, do the laundry, and help with schoolwork all in the same hour. My hat is off to the moms who invented multitasking; office personnel are still trying to figure it out.

I must treat my wife as an heir together with me of the grace of life. We are sharing this journey; it's not all about me. This is where Abraham missed it. He knew he was an heir of God's favor himself, but he failed to include his wife at first. He dragged her from place to place, willing to sell her to any king that wanted her so he would not lose his own sorry hide. After all, he had to preserve himself so the promise would come. Finally, he realized they were to inherit all of God's promises together. Everything God has in store for me is for my wife to enjoy as well. I do not want to leave her behind while I chase my destiny. She is part of my destiny.

Off-balance marriages suffer hindered prayers. Husbands, if we do not properly honor, cherish, nurture, defend, include, and provide for our wives, our prayers will not prosper either. Just as hair length is an indicator of a person's recognition of how God created them, so how one handles marriage is an indication of how one understands Christ and the church. If I misuse my marriage, I do not really know the Master and I misalign myself from the blessings in store for my home.

Have you ever wondered why Adam took the most heat from God about the first sin? Adam was the head, the beginning of the home. Perhaps he did not build his wife up with God's Word about the seriousness of the situation.[15] Yes, his wife was blindsided into sinning,[16] but he was the head, the source of that relationship. While there are exceptions, the weight of responsibility falls on the head in the marriage today, too.

OVERCOME THE CURSE

No Bible passage tells the man to boss his wife around. A nurturing, cherishing husband leads his home in the right path without having to be domineering. When Pentecost came to Latin America, women in a rather subjugating culture rejoiced because the men became more faithful to their spouses, focused more attention on the home, and became nurturers in both family and church.[17]

Part of the curse was bossiness from the husband. God told Eve:

> "Your desire shall be for your husband, And he shall rule over you" (Genesis 3:16).

This was not normal behavior for either of them but it is sinful behavior.

Just as we look for ways to lighten man's load from the curse of exhausting labor and we look for ways to ease a woman's pain in childbirth, so we should look for ways to reduce the curse of a husband ruling over his wife. Of course, every man wants a wife to desire him, but that is not what appears to be the original sense of that word when the Lord spoke it. God used some of these same words when talking to Cain, which will help us understand better.

God also told Cain about the sin crouching at his door:

> "its desire is for you, but you should rule over it" (Genesis 4:7).

Sin desired Cain in a controlling, destructive way. The effects of sin can lead to a desire to control and manipulate other people. Cain was instructed to rule over sin which parallels how sinful Adam would rule his woman. Of course it is right that people would rule over sin, but God did not say Adam should domineer his woman, but that the effects of sin would cause him to.

Husband, do you rule your wife the way you should rule over sin? I hope not. While you take authority over sinful impulses, you are a twisted man if you control and manipulate a woman. Wife, do you desire to control your husband the way sin desires to control you? If so, you are walking as a fallen human, not a daughter of Sarah. In keeping with the curse, both husband and wife will struggle against the urge to manipulate one another. Conflict is human; unity is divine. In the Lord Jesus, we are new creatures. Like Adam and Eve before their rebellion, we do not have to live under that curse.

MARRIED, IN MINISTRY

Some say a woman cannot be a pastor if she is not submitted to her husband. If that is true, then the reverse is true. A man should not be in ministry if he is not serving his wife, giving himself for her, and cherishing her.

> *A man should not be in ministry if he is not serving his wife, giving himself for her, and cherishing her.*

Some men cringe at the idea of being married to a woman who is outspoken as a preacher or a pastor. Would he lose his manhood to be in such a situation? To answer, let me illustrate how silly such worries are. I'm really intimidated by my wife. Last night she made the best home-cooked meal ever. It shamed me. I can barely fry eggs. Not only did she soak the meat in divine juices, but then she smoked it until it was saturated with flavor from fruit woods. I, who can only create messes in the kitchen, have to sit under the benevolence of her culinary expertise.

Sigh.

Of course, I am saying this all in jest. I love my wife's cooking and would rather not eat anywhere but at home.

What does this have to do with women in ministry? If a man's wife can serve up a spiritual feast, I say scoot up to the table, Mister, and dig in. If she has the talent, find the appetite. If she preaches revelatory truths, enjoy it rather than be intimidated. If a man is secure in His calling, he should respect his wife's calling.

Some husbands might worry about their wives having authority over them. I guess it is a little controlling of my wife to set out a specific meal. I am forced to eat what she makes—it is not like she cooks five different meals and leaves me the authority to choose what I want to eat. Is she controlling me? I want a menu! I want a choice! After all, I *am* the man of the house.

For another point of comparison, a married couple are both professors at a college. The woman becomes academic dean. Now, her husband is subject to her decisions. Who is submitted to whom? In the workplace, he will take his orders from her, not because of her gender or relationship with him but because of her level of leadership in the school. So at home, she would follow his leadership, but in their service to the learning community, he would follow hers.

Bernadine Caldwell served the Lord as both a pastor and evangelist. She said her husband was always accepting of her calling and never tried to hold her back. "He was secure in himself and not challenged by my ministry. I remember attending a ministers' meeting where they had all of the minister's spouses tell how they helped their husbands. I was the only woman preacher there. When they got to my husband he told them that he 'rubs her back and helps her find her glasses.'"[18]

It takes a big man to promote his wife. A man can be married to his pastor and still be very much man of the home. Her authority is not in her gender but from God. This might be easier to accept if a man married a woman who was already pastor of a church. If a man has dominated his wife in their prior years of marriage, this might be a difficult change of paradigm for him. How does he make that transition from being her master to being a team player? By becoming the husband he should have been in the first place.

He needs to give himself for her as Christ does the church. For those who understand servant-leadership, this bridge is not hard to cross. This revelation shocks men who think they were called by God to boss their wives around.

At one time, I was that kind of husband. Then I discovered that spouses share authority over one another. I Corinthians 7:4 says, "The wife does not have authority over her own body, but the husband does. And likewise the husband does not have authority over his own body, but the wife does."[19] So much for him dominating her or vice versa. In the most intimate area of marriage, the wife and husband share equal authority over one another. Such a relationship means that a disagreement must be resolved by mutual agreement, in other words as verse 5 says, making decisions "by consent."

Scripture never tells the pastor of a church to be lord over the congregants.[20] Some scholars make the mistake of applying the husband/wife roles to the church.[21] While it is true that both wives and church members are to submit to those in leadership, a husband needs to be a servant leader as much as a pastor leads in humility.

In perfect maturity, married partners will find oneness in Christ. Husbands learn to lead with gentle care and wives learn to follow with humble respect. My submissive wife sees her wishes fulfilled more than most domineering women I have seen. Because of her sweet spirit, I ask Leanne for her opinion and value her perspectives on issues. As a couple grows in the Lord, they will become a strong team. To those outside the marriage, they may look like equals. That is not the result of feminism or communism but humility. This is the same maturity we need in the church, workplace, and society. Harmony grows as each one rests in his or her position in the Lord and His calling on their lives.

God called E. L. and Nona Freeman separately to Africa. They were surprised to find that He had called them both to ministry together. God also called Carl and Mable Hensley to ministry overseas. Before she was married, Mable received a call to China. Sometime later,

> a missionary to China, Sister Addell Harrison and her daughter, were visiting in the Lowe home where the Hensleys were staying. One day out of nowhere Sister Harrison said to her, "Mable, why don't you two go to China with me?"
>
> "China!" Mable cried out. "Sister Harrison, China? I'm scared of the Chinese!" Immediately she heard a voice saying, "You didn't ask Me about this, did you?" Smitten in her heart by this question she knew was from the Lord, she turned and ran into her bedroom and threw herself across the bed weeping uncontrollably. After weeping and praying for quite some time, her husband came and putting his arm around her, said, "Honey, whatever the Lord is asking you to do, say yes!"
>
> Startled, she turned to him and asked, "Where did you come from?"
>
> "I was lying on the bed listening to you pray. I had been praying before you came in. Mable, if God wants us to be missionaries, we'll have to go. So both of us must say, 'yes.'" Kneeling at the bed together in humble submission and prayer, both knew they would be going to the mission field.
>
> A message in tongues and interpretation came in the missionary service that night: "Don't hesitate to accept My leading for it is I, God, Who is speaking to two people in this congregation tonight. You, to whom I am speaking, know who you are."
>
> As Mable listened to the interpretation, her experience the morning Brother Urshan had preached at their church while she was still unmarried, came back to her forcefully. She stood to her feet and said, "Yes we know who has been called. Carl and I must go to China!"[22]

May all husbands and wives be willing to do whatever the Lord asks of them.

The Lord did not give Adam a wife so she could go be team-partner to some other man. Eve was Adam's helpmeet or counterpartner, first. Though it took my wife and me years to figure it out after we married, He called us *together*. We are to be *united* in marriage. Our personal callings have to mesh into who we are as a team. I cannot pursue my own mission to her neglect. It is a challenge, but we work together to accomplish what He has set before us.

I thank God for a wife who has teamed up with me in my calling—she has become a ministry counterpartner to me. Many times she has counseled a wife in a situation while I counseled the husband. She is the practical person; I am the geek who needs to be balanced by her level-headedness. By bringing two pianos and a keyboard into our house, I have sought to support her music ministry as much as possible, as well. At the same time she encourages and supports my call to writing and teaching.

Some may find this blending of their calling with their spouse's as a difficulty. I see it as an art form. It takes creativity and a sense of adventure to fit into the callings of God together. It does not seem healthy for a marriage or for morals for a woman to absent herself from home and family to pursue her calling while the husband does the same in a different direction. A couple will do much to protect their marriage by working as a team. The Lord did not call you together to pull you apart.

TO MARRY OR NOT TO MARRY

Of course, one can quickly see in all of this Paul's point about the unmarried. If you are single, you are at much greater liberty to serve God. A marriage will almost always slow down a ministry at least through the learning phase of their becoming one. To those who thought marriage would solve everything, Paul warned that "such will have trouble in the flesh, but I would spare you."[23] Without marriages, however, God's people would never take part in one of the greatest missions on earth: children.

I do not see a higher calling than parenting. Nothing my wife and I do will be more important than the investment we make in our children. A mother cannot have a higher calling than to care for and raise up godly young people. If she is called to preach or build churches, God would not call her to do that to the neglect of her family. Too many missionaries lost their own children by sending them to boarding school while they did Kingdom work.

I would encourage every mother to add as much to the spiritual health of her home as possible. My mom did much work in teaching us and praying with us, and I remember hearing my father early in the morning, filling our home with an atmosphere of the Spirit. We sat down as a family to open the Bible together. Even if the husband is not a preacher, he needs to open the Word of God to his family. He needs to be the spiritual point of beginning (head) for them.

Because of our broken world, many families depend on the influence of the church for their children to find good role models and balance for what their home might be lacking. Children need godly female and male mentors for a proper understanding of gender roles. In a society where dads are perpetually absent, women often have to raise the young men. As I heard an NFL coach once say, because many men have left their boys to be raised by the women, they grow up to be men just like mom—complete with earrings and a ponytail.

Girls need moms to help them become ladies and not roughnecks. Boys need a godly female influence so they can learn how to treat a future wife. Girls need a godly male influence to teach them how to interact with men. Boys need dads who will let them try crazy things that moms would not tolerate, so young men learn their limits while still young (a topic big enough to be a book of its own, which is why I have written *Devotions with Dad*).

The best way to raise a family is to involve them in ministry. Sister Caldwell worried what effect a newborn would have on her ministry: "When I was 40 years old and had only been preaching for five years, my son Curtis was born. I thought perhaps my husband would object to my taking him to revivals, but the Lord intervened and again my husband was very considerate."[24] She rejoiced to be able to bring her son along in the ministry as she had her daughters.

When the Lord called my parents to do children's ministry, they included their children. We traveled all over North America for several years. My teen years were shaped by praying with children in the altar and ministering through playing drums and doing puppets, skits, and songs. Nothing has been more valuable to me in life than what I could do for the kingdom of God. Mothers and fathers must find where their callings include their children also. I cannot imagine what my life would have been had they left us behind.

All this talk about ministry and calling can make a woman feel left out if she is not a preacher. While this book seeks to help clarify a woman's place in ministry, I do not want to intimidate those who are not called to be out front. Ruth Senter shared her story of how women often feel in this age of feminism:

> Used to be, I decided for myself where my significance came from. I got my clues from God. But now other voices are trying to help me decide. And the impression I get is this: significant things for women can only happen in boardrooms, classrooms, courtrooms, newsrooms, or some such place.
>
> The irony is that some of the moments of my life when I've most sensed that what I'm doing may actually be leaving a legacy for eternity have occurred in my children's bedrooms or in our family room or around our kitchen table. Those have been the times I've looked

> into the faces of the ones I love and said to myself, "I am helping them become all they can be. Life doesn't get much better than this."
>
> But that was before the rumbling that *that* wasn't enough.[25]

If the worldly craze for money and success is making a woman feel insignificant, she should rest herself in the Lord and His calling for her. Jesus told Martha that Mary's sitting at His feet was enough. When others criticized her for not giving to the poor, He told them what she had done was enough. No believer needs to live in a continual state of "that's not enough."

The contentment of ministering within the home to children and husband can be more rewarding than any career or societal cause one might feel she has to fulfill. Senter continues,

> I picture my mother and dad holding hands across their recliners every morning when they have their prayer time together. And I feel the loss. Not for them, but for women everywhere who aren't content with their husbands anymore, who think it is old-fashioned to share your energy with a man.
>
> Whatever happened to the notion that marriage is a joint union of shared energy, shared surrendering up for the sake of another?[26]

Husband and wife, you are heirs together of this grace of life. Live it joyfully and watch God answer your prayers.

Husbands, help your wife find her place in ministry. The fields are ready for harvest, we have prayed for laborers, and we must now accept those the Master has called to work in the field. Ruth should not have to just glean the edges of the field.[27] The harvest is hers as much as anyone's.

12 | He Called Tabitha: Women as Role-models

Where does a woman get started in ministry?

At Joppa there was a certain disciple named Tabitha, which is translated Dorcas. This woman was full of good works and charitable deeds which she did. But it happened in those days that she became sick and died. When they had washed her, they laid her in an upper room. And since Lydda was near Joppa, and the disciples had heard that Peter was there, they sent two men to him, imploring him not to delay in coming to them. Then Peter arose and went with them.
When he had come, they brought him to the upper room. And all the widows stood by him weeping, showing the tunics and garments which Dorcas had made while she was with them. But Peter put them all out, and knelt down and prayed. And turning to the body he said, "Tabitha, arise." And she opened her eyes, and when she saw Peter she sat up. Then he gave her his hand and lifted her up; and when he had called the saints and widows, he presented her alive
(Acts 9:36–41).

Our girls need to see the power of God working in anointed women who are doing what the Lord has called them to do. This does not just mean pulpit ministry. Tabitha influenced the believers, but we do not read that she ever preached a sermon or taught a Bible study. However, she was such a dynamic woman that when she died, two men went running to the Apostle Peter to see if he could bring her back.

The name Tabitha means "gazelle."[1] She was graceful and did many things for the people of God. She made them clothes and may have even put together a quilt or two. She had a servant's heart and found ways to help wherever she went. People like her are hard to find and when you lose one, you want her back.

The apostle prayed and by the power of God she came back to life. She was not a preacher, but by this miracle, many in that area came to believe on the Lord. I wonder how much of an impact this might have had on Peter. He was the one who cursed at the servant girl on the eve of Christ's death. He is the one who did not believe Mary's words about Jesus until he saw the empty tomb for himself. Maybe just before his big learning experience with the Gentiles in Joppa, God was helping reset his value for women, too.

Tabitha was an elder and probably a widow because the widows appear to have been her closest friends. They stood weeping over the loss of this jewel of a woman who was full of good deeds. While not every woman will become a preacher, she should become a Tabitha. A godly elderly woman "trusts in God and continues in supplications and prayers night and day."[2]

A woman of God should live her life with dignity. While every woman is called to a godly reputation, not every woman should be a preacher. In some way, though, every woman in the Kingdom must influence the next generation to be examples of holiness, good mothers, and protectors of their homes (Titus 2:3–5). A godly woman may not preach a revival but can change the world by raising a Timothy. Both Lois and Eunice

> *Every woman in the Kingdom must influence the next generation to be examples of holiness, good mothers, and protectors of their homes.*

had this brilliant young leader as a feather in their hats. This happens by instruction but mainly by setting a godly example. Timothy would not have become the man he became without Paul as a father in the faith. However, Paul would not have been able to take him as far as he did without those two women giving him a scriptural foundation.

YOUR MINISTRY

The most important thing is to find your role and fulfill it. Whatever the Lord calls you to, remember this: your calling is not the most important thing that ever happened to you. Jesus is.

If Jesus has called you, He will open the doors for you—you do not have to force them open by human means. At the same time, do all you can to fulfill your ministry. You cannot push your way into a pulpit, but no pastor will forbid you from winning souls.

One of the most needed ministries today is that we have intercessors who will pray heaven-moving prayers. Billy Cole, missionary, pastor, and evangelist, saw thousands and thousands of people filled with the Spirit of God. He said, "One of the greatest advantages of my ministry was my wife's prayer life—daily."[3] When going into Indonesia for the first time she lay on the floor for hours in intercession. This area had only seen thirty-five people filled with the Holy Ghost within two years' time. Billy and Shirley Cole ministered in that land for twenty-one days and 657 souls received the baptism of the Spirit! Such occurrences were not unusual in their ministry.

They fought many spiritual battles alone. In this day, there should be no servant of the Lord who has to do kingdom work alone. As Paul sought, every great servant of God needs someone to "help together in prayer."[4] Travailing prayer is one of the most powerful and effective ministries one can do.

PACE YOURSELF

My wife gave birth to our first child with no one but me in attendance. Being young and adventurous, she decided to have a midwife deliver our child for us at home. Unfortunately, my wife is prone to what is called precipitous labor, which occurs in less than three hours. Her first warning signs were at 2:30 AM and she called the midwife. An hour later, the contractions were intense enough that the midwife picked up her two assistants and headed for our house.

Meanwhile, back at the ranch, I panicked not knowing what to do. The best I could figure was comb my hair so I would not look like a bedhead when the birth attendants arrived. Then I caught my firstborn son. Fortunately, they had trained us in the birthing classes what to do if we had to deliver on our own, and we did all right.

Precipitous labor can be hard on both the baby and the mother. She needs to transition slowly and not get in such a hurry. Without having time to adjust to the process properly, my wife had some healing to do after that rough start at motherhood.[5]

With that in mind, I say again, one should not rush into ministry. Men, you might get inspired and want to see women prosper under your ministry, but do not push a woman into the pulpit to make it happen. Ministries are like babies and they do best through a normal birthing process. Ladies, if you are called to lead, do not push things too quickly. The apostles spent three years in training before leading. I wonder if anything less than that could be called "precipitous ministry." Transition through your time as a servant, prayer warrior, and soulwinner before you take the role of overseer. God will set before you an open door as He is ready. The most important door is already open: the door to lost souls.

> *Transition through your time as a servant, prayer warrior, and soulwinner before you take the role of overseer.*

If you are a woman who thought you could not be in the ministry, reading this book may have been a whirlwind for you. Perhaps you are still adjusting to the idea that God wants to use you. If that is the case, then rushing out to do a ministry might be precipitous, pushing things too quickly for you.

ADAPTING TO A NEW PARADIGM

One of the concerns I have when people have been taught that a certain thing is unbiblical is that changing the old norm too quickly may destabilize their faith. For example, a generation ago, old-style nylons had a seam up the back. One Bible school taught against wearing hosiery without a seam. Now, if they had said this was a biblical command, it could have been destabilizing to someone's faith when they found out the Bible says nothing about women's stockings, especially now that the seamed variety are virtually non-existent. Such a conviction preached as a doctrine could cause a weak believer to question everything else they had been taught about modesty or morality when they discover it was non-biblical.

I fear the same results from those who have forced their own opinions against women in ministry and claimed that they were biblical. If a man has an opinion on a thing, it is fair for him to share it as a personal perspective. However, saying something is from God when it is not will ultimately damage another's faith. Paul said to be careful with others' beliefs. If they felt it was a sin to eat meat, then do not force them to eat meat or even eat it in front of them. The concern is that if you injure their weak faith, they might throw out all of what little they have.[6]

The issue of women in ministry is slightly different than observing holidays or eating food sacrificed to idols. This is not a take-it-or-leave-it option in life. Whether a woman or man responds to his or her calling from God has everything to do with that individual's life purpose and possibly salvation.

We cannot reject the idea of women in ministry for fear of injuring the faith of a weak brother. This is a different issue. The solution then? To teach. What strengthens those weak in the faith is the teaching of truth.

The Lord will hold women responsible who do not obey His call on their lives. Could He also hold the men responsible who prevent women from answering the call on their lives? What about the souls who could have been won or strengthened by a woman minister? Who will answer for them, if she is not allowed to obey God's call on her life?

At the same time, God will make a way for those whom He has called. I have a friend who went many years from the time he first expressed his desire to be a preacher until he was finally given the opportunity to do so. He did not become resentful or try to start a ministry on his own. Instead, he got involved in everything the church had going on—organizing church cleanup days and serving the pastor in every other way possible. Finally, as he neared senior citizen status, he was able to start preaching. All those years of faithfully serving and patiently waiting for God to open the door saw him reap a great harvest from his labors. In the few short years he has been ministering and preaching, he has ministered to hundreds and hundreds who received the Holy Ghost. It is as if he is making up for lost time. God did not forget him even if things did not happen the way he had hoped.

FIND YOUR PLACE

My wife has a couple favorite places I take her that do steak right. When we eat steak, we like marinated meat that has been slowly cooked. I am not much of a chef, but I know that my hurried attempts at making food only turn out tough steaks that are miserable to chew.

Leaders are similar. Some have been through things that softened them, broke down any hardness, and developed wisdom in them over a number of years. Others are tough and harsh, putting a bad taste in your mouth. Leaders, like steaks, often start out equal. What distinguishes them is their process of development. In the kingdom of God, we need leaders who have slowly developed the rich flavor of strong morals, integrity, and compassion toward others. Like Deborah, a leader must develop depth of character before hitting the limelight.

Remember, some may be slower to accept your calling than others. If you want a place to preach, volunteer to start a new church plant (if that is what the Lord would have you do). On some mission fields you might have more acceptance than in the West, but in certain other countries a female preacher might receive significantly less respect. Even as a man, I have faced opposition from those who did not want to follow my leadership. That was a lot harder to work through than just teaching and preaching as a helper in the church. Everyone goes through season(ing)s and just being called does not make ministry easy.

Give yourself to the work He has called you to do. The disciples were unlikely leaders in Jerusalem but they turned the whole world upside down because they let the Lord work through them, in spite of rejection. What others will respect is someone who has obviously "been with Jesus."

At the same time, we need more Pauls who are willing to send a Phoebe in their place. We need to trust another Lydia with leading a flock. We must have more Junias and Priscillas risking their lives and taking the heat for the gospel. Most of all, we need Annas, Sarahs, and Tabithas who set the mold for the next generation of fervent believers.

Deborah did not clamor for a position, she just lived with such integrity and character others sought her out for advice. They asked her to lead. Walk in the Spirit, let the Lord live through you, and fulfill your calling.

WELL-SEASONED LEADERS

I remember once being on a low point in my spiritual journey and a Tabitha picked me up. She did not come at me with any words of correction or give me the scolding I needed. When others whom I looked up to just looked away, she spoke respectfully to me. She treated me as if I was better than she was and that amazed me. When I was needing a talking (down) to, she talked up to me and made me feel worthwhile as a person. Of course she was much closer to the Lord than I was: she was serving God, passionate about His kingdom, following His will. I was running from God's will for my life and bucking against my leaders, yet she elevated me. As I listened to her uplifting words, she renewed my vision of what the Lord wanted to do in my life. Over everything said and done from the pulpit at that camp meeting, she did more for me. She hardly knew me. She wasn't even a preacher.

It is time for another Tabitha generation to arise. It seems the art of being an aged woman in the Lord is being lost in a world where women are ashamed of the gray in their hair. Rather than celebrate their golden years, women are feeling pressured by society to cling to an image of youth. I rejoice when I see a congregation of believers with several heads full of the white hair of wisdom. Usually this means there are prayer warriors and good counselors to keep the body strong. Revival churches are fired by intercessors who give themselves to groaning travail. While many look to the youth department to be the lifeblood of the church, I have found the elderly to be the backbone of righteousness and the mature influence that will keep the church on track.

We need experienced mothers and grandmothers who will teach the young ladies how to be a good counterpartner to their husbands, to order their homes, and bring up godly children (Titus 2:4). They need more examples of women of God who live out His calling. Even as a young mother

Joy Haney would kneel in prayer in the children's play room while the youngsters played and climbed across her back.

CHANGE OF PARADIGM

As this book has shown from Scripture, it is apostolic to have female apostles, female prophets, female evangelists, female pastors, female teachers, and many women of God speaking for Him with spiritual gifts. I have looked at all sides of the debates regarding Scriptures that might pertain to the role of women in ministry and have presented them to the best of my understanding in this book.

For those who have read this book yet remain unconvinced about women as teachers and pastors, I understand that deep-seated teachings may be hard to see past after a lifetime of believing them. After hearing a woman preach, one pastor came away saying, "I used to not believe in women preachers. Now I do." I am not sure this or any other book could be more convincing than seeing the hand of God work mightily through a sister He has called.

The calling of God gives a human a purpose in life. When I was sixteen years old, I remember sitting in the balcony at a camp meeting, listening to Lloyd Squires preach to the children. The Spirit of God was moving in that room and penetrated my mixed-up turmoil of searching for purpose in life. I knew I was supposed to serve God with my life, but I was not sure how. At that moment, Jesus called me to write for Him. It was such a confirming moment for me.

I cannot imagine someone telling me back then that teenage guys could not write. I wonder how I would take it if someone told me today that God does not want bald guys to publish books anymore. I would find that insulting and demeaning. I have always defined prejudice as treating a person a certain way because of things they cannot change. I cannot change my baldness; I have surely tried. I can change sinfulness. I can change poor grammar. But I cannot change what God has called me to be: a child of God who writes for Him.

God has called many women to many forms of ministry. When the Lord calls my daughters to serve Him in some way, I hope no one tells them they cannot because of their gender. The Lord only asks us to change the things we can change, behaviors, for example. He does not fault us for the way He created us. He not only created women as a reflection of His image, but He also called them to serve Him. The concept behind the complex discussions in this book is simple: a woman can serve God because *He Called Her.*

So, "as each one has received a gift, minister it to one another, as good stewards of the manifold grace of God." If one is called to speak, he or she must "speak as the oracles of God" so that "in all things God may be glorified through Jesus Christ" (I Peter 4:10–11). If I listen to an anointed preacher, male or female, I should be hearing the voice of God. I must not listen to the gender but the Sender.

The disciples listened to the women who had been to the tomb, Timothy got his faith from the women in his life, Apollos changed his preaching at the teaching of Priscilla, and hundreds of first-century believers benefited from the ministries of Junia, Mary, Phoebe, Chloe, and so many more. Today, so many have prospered from the words of Vesta Mangun, Joy Haney, Janice Sjostrand, Nancy Grandquist, Vani Marshall, Oma Ellis, and countless other ladies of the Lord. Not every woman will be a preacher or pastor, but every woman has a ministry.

Women's lips heralded both the beginning and ending of Jesus' work on earth. Elizabeth and Anna announced Jesus' birth. Mary Magdalene and Joanna were among the women to first proclaim Jesus' resurrection. Our Lord who inspired women to speak for Him then encourages them to do the same today.

Notes

CHAPTER 1
HE CALLED JUNIA: WOMEN AS MISSIONARIES

1. All Scripture quotations are from the New King James Version, unless otherwise noted.
2. Actually, it was God's original plan for all Israel to be a kingdom of priests. Although it would take longer to develop than would serve the purposes of this writing, it appears the institution of the Levite priesthood came as a result of the people rejecting that personal approach to God as individuals. See Exodus 3:12; 19:6, 16; Deuteronomy 5:5.
3. Craig S. Keener, "Women in ministry: another egalitarian perspective," *Two Views on Women in Ministry*, rev. ed., James R. Beck, ed. (Grand Rapids, MI: Zondervan, 2005), 208.
4. Stanley J. Grenz, *Women in the Church: A Biblical Theology of Women in Ministry* (Downers Grove, IL: InterVarsity, 1995), 181–82 quoting Eileen Vennum, "Do Male Old Covenant Priests Exclude Female New Covenant Pastors?," Priscilla Papers 7, no. 2 (Spring 1993): 6–7.
5. Hebrews 5:6, 10; 6:20; 7:11, 17, 21.
6. Wayne Grudem, *Evangelical Feminism & Biblical Truth: An Analysis of More than 100 Disputed Questions*, Revised (Wheaton, IL: Crossway, 2012), 224.
7. Keener, "Women," 212. In Romans 1:13 and 8:29, Paul declares how he wanted to bear fruit among the readers and how Jesus became firstborn among many brethren. These parallel phrases to "of note among the apostles" indicate Junia being significant within the group called apostles, not the group of apostles simply taking note of her.
8. Juli Jasinski, *Step Up—For Lady Preachers ONLY* (Hollis, NH: 2013), unnumbered insert between pages 38–39.
9. Ben Witherington and Darlene Hyatt, *Paul's Letter to the Romans: A Socio-Rhetorical Commentary* (Grand Rapids, MI: Eerdmans, 2004), 390. and n. 65.
10. Witherington and Hyatt, *Paul's Letter to the Romans*, 390, quoting Clark "Jew and Greek," 119.
11. Richard Bauckham, *Gospel Women* (Grand Rapids, MI: Eerdmans, 2002), 179.
12. Witherington and Hyatt, *Paul's Letters to the Romans*, 389.

13. I Corinthians 15:7.
14. Bauckham, *Gospel Women*, 165–202.
15. Ben Witherington, *Women and the Genesis of Christianity* (New York: Cambridge, 1990), 188. See Luke 10:1; I Corinthians 9:6. While all of this is too sketchy to say for sure, perhaps married couples could have gone out to minister in teams of two even during Jesus' day like when He sent the seventy.
16. Luke 24:10.
17. Junia was probably not the only female apostle. Paul referred to Euodia, Syntyche, and Priscilla as *fellow-laborers* (Romans 16:3; Philippians 4:2–3), a term also used in reference to Epaphroditus, Timothy, Titus, and others (Romans 16:3; II Corinthians 8:23; Philippians 2:25; 4:3; Colossians 4:11; I Thessalonians 3:2; Philemon 1:24). These who were laboring alongside the apostle were doing apostle work. Paul referred to such co-laborers with the word apostles as well (II Corinthians 8:23; Philippians 2:25. While translated as "messengers," the level of commitment of these workers proves they were more than water boys.). If fellow-laborer with an apostle means one is an apostle, then Euodia, Syntyche, and Priscilla were also apostles.
18. Bill Drost, *Bill Drost The Pentecost* (Hazelwood, MO: Word Aflame: 1983), 114–17.
19. Susan Hill Lindley, *"You Have Stept Out of Your Place"* (Louisville, KY: Westminster John Knox, 1996), 4–5.
20. Ibid., 10.
21. Ruth A. Tucker, *First Ladies of the Parish* (Grand Rapids, MI: Zondervan, 1988), 56.
22. Ibid., 56–59.
23. Ibid., 46–47, emphasis original.
24. Lindley, *You Have Stept Out of Your Place*, 66, referencing Anne M. Boylan, "Evangelical Womanhood in the Nineteenth Century: The Role of Women in Sunday Schools," *Feminist Studies* 4, Oct 1978: 62–80.
25. Ibid., 68–69, quoting Leonard Sweet.
26. Ian Randall, *Rhythms of Revival: The Spiritual Awakening of 1857–63* (Milton Keynes, UK: Paternoster, 2010), 61.
27. Lindley, *You Have Stept Out of Your Place*, 79.
28. Ibid., 87.
29. Prathia Hall Wynn, "Foreword," *Those Preachin' Women: Sermons by Black Women Preachers*, Ella Pearson Mitchell, ed. (Valley Forge, VA: Judson, 1985), 12–13.
30. J. Edwin Orr, *The Fervent Prayer* (Chicago, IL: Moody, 1974), 96.
31. Ibid., 97.
32. James L. Tyson, *The Early Pentecostal Revival* (Hazelwood, MO: Word Aflame, 1992), 29.
33. Tyson, *The Early Pentecostal Revival*, 132.
34. Lindley, *You Have Stept Out of Your Place*, 330.
35. Susan C. Hyatt, "Spirit-Filled Women," *Century of the Holy Spirit*, Vinson Synan, ed. (Nashville, TN: Thomas Nelson, 2001), 233–264. Norris, "Glass Ceiling," 7, cites Grant Wacker, *Heaven Below: Early Pentecostals and American Culture* (Cambridge MA: Harvard University, 2001), as quoting Emma Cotton's claim that Lucy Farrow was "the central prophet igniting the Holy Ghost fires in Southern California."
36. Tyson, *The Early Pentecostal Revival*, 131–32.
37. Ibid., 139.
38. Mark Shaw, *Global Awakening: How 20th-Century Revivals Triggered a Christian Revolution* (Downers Grove, IL: InterVarsity, 2010), 22–23.
39. Barbara Bair, "'Ethiopia Shall Stretch Forth Her Hands unto God': Laura Kofey and the Gendered Vision of Redemption in the Garvey Movement," *A Mighty Baptism: Race, Gender, and the Creation of American Protestantism*, Susan Juster and Lisa MacFarlane, eds. (Ithaca, NY: Cornell, 1996), 48.
40. Tyson, *The Early Pentecostal Revival*, 137–38.
41. Lindley, *You Have Stept Out of Your Place*, 333.
42. Ibid., 10.

43. David K. Bernard, "Women in Ministry," *Pentecostal Herald*, Sept 2012, 6.
44. David Norris, "Glass Ceiling: Women Who Minister," Urshan Graduate School Symposium, Hazelwood, MO, 2007, 8.
45. Georgia Smelser, *Oma* (Hazelwood, MO: Word Aflame, 1981), 198–200.
46. Lindley, *You Have Stept Out of Your Place*, 476–77, n. 23 references Charles H. Barfoot and Gerald T. Sheppard, "Prophetic vs. Priestly Religion: The Changing Role of Women Clergy in Classical Pentecostal Churches," *RRR* 22 (September 1980): 4.
47. Ibid., 334–35.
48. Leland E. Wilshire, *Insight into Two Biblical Passages* (Lanham, Mar: University, 2010), 42, quoting Max Weber, *The Sociology of Religion*, trans. by Ephraim Fischoff (Boston Beacon, 1922, 1963), 104.
49. Bernard, *The Apostolic Life* (Hazelwood, MO: Word Aflame, 2006), 250.
50. Lindley, *You Have Stept Out of Your Place*, 329.
51. Gail Bederman, "'The Women Have Had Charge of the Church Work Long Enough': The Men and Religion Forward Movement of 1911–1912 and the Masculinization of Middle-Class Protestantism," *A Mighty Baptism*, Juster and MacFarlane, eds. (Ithaca, NY: Cornell, 1996), 107–11.
52. Bederman, "The Women," 138, and Linda McKinnish Bridges, "Women in Church Leadership," *RevExp*, 95, Aug 1 1998, 336.
53. Bederman, "The Women,"138.
54. Ibid.
55. Vinson Synan, *The Holiness-Pentecostal Movement in the United States* (Grand Rapids, MI: Eerdmans, 1971), 188.
56. Lindley, *You Have Stept Out of Your Place*, 62.
57. Ibid., 63.

CHAPTER 2

HE CALLED MARY: WOMEN AS EVANGELISTS

1. Luke 13:20, 15:8; 17:35.
2. Scholars debate whether Mary Magdalene was the sister Mary of Martha or a different Mary. That is a valid discussion, but for the purpose of this chapter, we are going to speak of her as one and the same Mary. Whether it was two women or one, the points raised by these Mary stories show much we can learn about women in ministry.
3. Janice Sjostrand, "A Woman's View of the Cross and the Resurrection," *Pentecostal Herald*, Apr 2011, 49.
4. In a sense, Mary in the garden toppled what Eve had done in the garden. Where the deceived woman reached out for the forbidden fruit, the faith-filled Mary reached out for the Master. Where angels had driven the first Adam and his wife out the entrance of the garden, angels opened the door for the Second Adam to join His wife, the Bride of Christ. Where Eve mistook the serpent for someone to trust and forsook her gardener husband, Mary mistook the trustworthy One for being a gardener. Where Eve had come under the bondage of the evil one, Mary had been set free forever from seven evil spirits. Where Eve had spoken out of turn, Jesus told Mary to speak for Him to the preachers He had trained who were now struggling with fear and doubt.
5. Revelation 12:12–14. The twelve disciples, however, were not likely from each of the twelve tribes because most of them came from one location. It was a spiritual heritage, not physical.
6. Matthew 19:28; also Luke 22:30.
7. Craig Keener, "A Response to Craig Blomberg," *Two Views*, 186.
8. Linda L. Belleville, *Women Leaders and the Church* (Grand Rapids, MI: Baker, 2000), 24.

9. Luke 4:18.
10. Luke 4:23–27.
11. Keener, *Paul*, 84.
12. Matthew 13:31–33; 24:37–41.
13. Joachim Jeremias, *Jerusalem in the Time of Jesus* (Philadelphia, PA: Fortress, 1969), 375–76.
14. Matthew 20:20; Mark 15:41; Luke 8:1–3.
15. Jeremias, *Jerusalem in the Time of Jesus*, 376.
16. I would not argue that the gospel writers, Paul, or even Jesus had an agenda to liberate women. Everyone was socially, religiously, and spiritually oppressed.
17. Exodus 15:20–21; 38:8; I Samuel 2:22; Luke 2:36–37.
18. Bauckham, *Gospel Women*, 110–21.
19. Keener, *Acts: An Exegetical Commentary*, Vol. 1 (Grand Rapids, MI: Baker, 2012), 600.
20. Matthew 28:1–8; Mark 16:1–11; Luke 24:9–12; John 20:1–18.
21. Luke 24:11.
22. Ethel E. Goss, *The Winds of God*, revised by Ruth Goss Nortjé (Hazelwood, MO: Word Aflame, 1977), 137.
23. Lindley, *You Have Stept Out of Your Place*, 124, quoting research from Frances Willard.
24. Ibid., 329.
25. Tucker, *First Ladies of the Parish*, 66, emphasis original.
26. Ibid., 68–69.
27. Randall, *Rhythyms of Revival*, 64. These included Caroline Reynolds, Janice Holmes, Eliza Haynes, Anne Davis, Pamela Shephard, Rose Clapham, Jenney Smith, and others.
28. Ibid., 61–62.
29. Ibid., 62.
30. Ibid.
31. Lindley, *You Have Stept Out of Your Place*, 333–34.
32. The root meaning of evangelist (*euaggelistēs*) implies someone who shares the gospel message with those who have not heard.
33. Adapted from Knofel Stanton, *The Biblical Liberation of Women for Leadership in the Church* (Eugene, OR: Wipf and Stock, 2003), 51–52.
34. Ruth A. Tucker, *Women in the Maze: Questions & Answers on Biblical Equality* (Downers Grove, IL: InterVarsity, 1992), 81.
35. Nona Freeman, *Everything Is Gonna Be All Right* (Fort Worth, TX: 2005), 61–62.
36. I Corinthians 1:26; James 2:5.

CHAPTER 3

HE CALLED ANNA: WOMEN AS PROPHETS

1. Rachel Cole, "Malinda Cole Montgomery," *Pioneer Pentecostal Women*, Vol. 2, Mary H. Wallace, ed. (Hazelwood, MO: Word Aflame, 1981), 154–56.
2. Calvinism is the theological teaching that follows John Calvin, a reformer from 16th century Geneva. He called for and supported the martyrdom of One-God defender Michael Servetus whom the Spanish Inquisition burned to death. Calvin popularized the idea of what is commonly called "eternal security." Calvinism teaches that God predestines individuals for salvation; so, Jesus did not die for everyone. It also teaches that God chooses souls and they cannot resist Him; so, they will be saved regardless of their will. This theological system has become popular again as Reformed Theology, promoted by such men as R. C. Sproul, John MacArthur, Wayne Grudem, and John Piper. Wayne Grudem is a Reformed Theologian who has become very outspoken against women in leadership and teaching. While his concerns are worth considering, his exegesis of key biblical passages about women has been tainted by his bias.

3. Luke 1:41–55; Acts 21:8; I Corinthians 11:3.
4. Wilshire, *Insight into Two Biblical Passages*, 61.
5. In Luke 1:19, 20, 22, this is the same word *laleō* that Paul used in I Corinthians 14:34–35.
6. Robin Johnston, Lee Ann Alexander, eds., *Apostolic Study Bible* (Hazelwood, Mo: Word Aflame, 2014), note for I Corinthians 14:34–35.
7. Grudem, *Evangelical Feminism & Biblical Truth*, 2012.
8. From the Greek word *sigaō*.
9. I Corinthians 12:8–10.
10. We have no record of Paul asking any women anywhere to silence their voices. Why would he demand this now? Instead, he is dealing with some heavy-duty issues in the group, including gender distinction in a believer's hair, proper observance of the Lord's Supper, and functioning in the gifts of the Spirit. This "women in silence" issue arises in the discussion of spiritual gifts.
11. Frequently the Bible quotes the bad guys such as Goliath and Herod. Scripture even quotes Satan but we know not to follow his words. We see the words of Job's friends but realize they were called to account before God for their judgmental statements. Therefore, we understand I Corinthians 14:34–35 in the proper context as Paul quotes the contenders in Corinth. He then responds to their thinking.
12. This is a euphemism for sexual behavior.
13. *King James Version*. The NKJV of this passage reads "Or did the word of God come originally from you?"
14. Gilbert Bilzekian, *Beyond Sex Roles*, Third edition (Grand Rapids, MI: Baker Academic, 2006), 115.
15. Metzger says that in codex Fuldensis a scribal marking sets out verses 34-35 almost as if the reader is to skip from verse 33 and continue reading at 36, Metzger, 499–500. Perhaps this was just a scribe's bias. However, could it have been an attempt to alert the reader to indicate that these two verses were a block quote? This much is certain, several other manuscripts also put a signal marking on these two verses as well. Perhaps more study on this would help confirm that these two verses were indeed a quote from the Corinthians' letter.
16. In the same book, see how he quotes Scriptures in I Corinthians. 2:16; 5:13; 10:26, 28; 15:27, 32 without introducing them.
17. I Corinthians 6:12–13. These may have been Corinthian clichés that excused sexual immorality.
18. David W. Odell-Scott, "In Defense of an Egalitarian Interpretation of I Corinthians 14:34–36: A Reply to Murphy-O'Connor's Critique," *BTB*, vol. 17 no. 3, 1987, 100.
19. The phrase, "in the churches," could be "in the assemblies" or "in the meetings." The Greek word *ekklēsia* means a meeting of people and could apply to a church or synagogue.
20. There might have been some Jewish politics involved. We know a ruler of the Jewish synagogue joined in this church's early history, as did a few other Jews (Acts 18). Perhaps Crispus or Justus tried to push their Jewish custom of silencing women in the assembly. Paul quotes their argument back to them before he refutes it.
21. Mary Hayter, *The New Eve in Christ: The Use and Abuse of the Bible in the Debate about Women in the Church* (Grand Rapids, MI: Eerdmans, 1987), 130, citing Barrett, *A Commentary on the First Epistle to the Corinthians*, 322.
22. Acts 7:60; 8:1–3; 9:2.
23. I Corinthians 9:10; 14:21. Paul used the law to illustrate truths in the new covenant, but spoke against living by the letter of the law.
24. Romans 7:6; Galatians 2:16; 3:25; 5:1.
25. Mark 7:3, 8. Pharisees and others who added to the Law of Moses were some of the most power-hungry people in Jesus' day. See also Matthew 15:2; 21:23–27; 23:2–6, 15–24; Mark 7:5–13; Luke 20:8, 46–47.
26. Charles Trombley, *Who Said Women Can't Teach?* (South Plainfield, NJ: Bridge, 1985), 24–25.

27. Trombley, *Who Said Women Can't Teach?*, 31; *Babylonian Talmud, Kiddushin* 1, 11.
28. Ibid., 29; *Apion II*, 201.
29. Jon Zens, *What's with Paul and Women?: Unlocking the Cultural Background to 1 Timothy 2* (Lincoln, NE: Ekklesia, 2010), 105, quoting Johann F. Schleusner's Greek-Latin Lexicon.
30. Trombley, *Who Said Women Can't Teach?*, 29, in *Tosephta Berakhoth* 7, 8; *Palestinian Talmud Berakhoth* 13b; *Babylonian Talmud Menakhoth* 43b.
31. Ibid., 31; *Babylonian Talmud, Kiddushin* 1, 11; *Berakhoth* 4, 36; *Mishnah Aboth* 1, 5.
32. Ibid., 31, *Mishnah Shabbath* 4, 1; *Sifre D.* 19:17.
33. Ibid., 34, *Babylonian Talmud, Berakhoth* 24a; *Shabbath* 64b; *Ned* 20a.
34. Several hints let us know these are not Paul's sentiments. The phrase, "ask their own husbands at home," does not sound like an apostle of Jesus Christ. Would Jesus tell someone to go figure things out at home? If there were confusion in the congregation, they needed teaching, not censure. Jesus used interruptions as teachable moments, not a reason to silence people. It seems neither biblical nor loving to send people home because they do not understand. It does, however, sound like first-century Judaism to silence women. It also seems like a Jewish tendency to assume that the women were married (Bilzekian, 114). Paul did not assume that all women would be married, nor did he pressure all women to marry. In fact, he applauds singleness earlier in this epistle (7:34–35). It is also a signal of Jewish thought that the man would be able to teach his wife the faith because all the Jewish men learned the scriptures. Since Gentile men and women would have been coming into an understanding of the one true God together, it does not seem logical that they would be the ones pushing this idea of unlearned husbands teaching wives. Again, all clues point to this being a Jewish statement.
35. Trombley, *Who Said Women Can't Teach?*, 34, *Babylonian Talmud, Kiddushin*, 70a.
36. Bilzekian, *Beyond Sex Roles*, 111.
37. Trombley, *Who Said Women Can't Teach?*, 32.
38. Zens, *What's with Paul and Women?*, 99; *Talmud, Tractate Kiddushin*.
39. Trombley, *Who Said Women Can't Teach?*, 34; *Babylonian Talmud, Berakhoth* 24a; *Shabbath* 64b.
40. The Greek word is *aischron*.
41. I Corinthians 11:6; Ephesians 5:11–12.

CHAPTER 4
HE CALLED DEBORAH: WOMEN AS LEADERS

1. Rebecca G. S. Idestrom, "Deborah: A Role Model for Christian Public Ministry," *Women, Ministry and the Gospel: Exploring New Paradigms*, Mark Husbands and Timothy Larsen, eds. (Downers Grove, IL: InterVarsity, 2007), 24.
2. See I Samuel 9:6–10. Craig S. Keener, *Paul, Women and Wives* (Grand Rapids, MI: Zondervan, 1992), 244.
3. Crystal Micko, "Interview with David Norris about *Cara's Call*," *Pentecostal Herald*, Sept 2012, 23. W. T. Witherspoon also reportedly never allowed his wife Jet, who was a minister, to preach in his own pulpit where he pastored.
4. Keener, "Women in Ministry: Another Egalitarian Perspective," *Two Views*, 211.
5. Some say the $\bar{e}$ at the beginning of the verse should be translated "What?" others say it should be "Or...?" Belleville, "Women," 73, n. 107, says that although "the particle $\bar{e}$ can express disapproval, it is a double $\bar{e}\bar{e}$ that functions in this way and not the single $\bar{e}$ found in 11:36." Once again, the definition depends on the context. However, if the $\bar{e}$ is not a negative response, the phrase "Or did the word of God come originally from you" does not fit as an optional statement to the preceding material or a logical construction in harmony with the preceding two verses. The context itself, not just the one particle, indicate the conflicting values. Grudem, 240, says this $\bar{e}$ negates

the following material in its other uses in the book. However, verse 36 negates both the preceding content and the following. Paul here raises the rhetorical questions of whether these people were the source of all God's revelation. Of course the answer is negative. In that case, his use of *ē* here is consistent with its usage in 6:15–16, 18–19; 9:4–6; 10:21–22 as well. In each of these instances, two ideologies are in conflict. Paul argues from extremes to prove a point. Therefore we can conclude, with Odell-Scott, "Defense," 102, "Beginning with the particle *e* and continuing with the negative rhetorical questions of v 36, he replies. His reply silenced (at least for a time) those who would silence women in church. Paul's position was clear: women are to speak in church."

6. Pronouns in the Greek can reflect the gender of the person(s) indicated. If he wanted to specifically chastise the women, one would have expected to see him reference only females here.

7. Neal M. Flanagan and Edwina H. Synder, "Did Paul Put Down Women in I Cor 14:34–36?" *BTB*, 11 (1981): 10.

8. Kenneth E. Bailey, *Paul Through Mediterranean Eyes: Cultural Studies in 1 Corinthians* (Downers Grove, Ill: InterVarsity, 2011), 411–18. Bailey presents Paul's handling of the church conflicts in a chiasmus beginning with chapter 11 and ending with chapter 14 which puts the principles of love (the greatest commandment) at the center of the entire discussion. A chiasmus is an outline showing matching elements which form a mirror image of the beginning of a passage to the end. The visual effect of this literary device, created by the author and recognized by the scholar, emphasizes the central portion of the text. So Paul's "commands of the Lord" in I Corinthians 14:37 are that they love one another, as described in I Corinthians 13:4–8a. The command to manage the church behavior correctly is tied to the character of love all believers must have toward one another.

9. The text reflects the author's loose paraphrase for emphasis. The exact circumstances in Corinth may never be recovered, but this is a realistic summary of what was happening in that location. No matter how one reads I Corinthians 14:34–35, it is abusive to the biblical text to use this passage to prevent women from ministry when no other passage silences women from talking.

10. Odell-Scott, "Let the Women Speak in Church: An Egalitarian Interpretation of I Cor. 14:33b–36," *BTB*, 13, 1983, 93.

11. Judges 4:17–22; 5:24–27.

12. From the Hebrew *shaphat*: to act as law-giver, judge, or governor; to decide a controversy or bring punishment.

13. Nona Freeman, "The Story of Mae Iry," *Profiles of Pentecostal Missionaries*, Mary H. Wallace, ed. (Hazelwood, MO: Word Aflame, 1986), 149–51.

CHAPTER 5
HE CALLED PRISCILLA: WOMEN AS TEACHERS

1. Georgia Smelser, *Oma* (Hazelwood, MO: Word Aflame, 1981), 26–30.

2. I Corinthians 16:19 mentions *their* house, as emphasized by Gordon Fee as "sure evidence that something has been transformed by the gospel." Norris, "Glass Ceiling," 1.

3. Acts 18:2; I Corinthians 16:19. In the passage in Acts 18:26 there is some discussion about whether Priscilla's name should come first or not. The KJV and NKJV follow the tradition that puts Aquila before Priscilla while versions based on the critical text put Priscilla before Aquila.

4. Acts 18:18; Romans 16:3; II Timothy 4:19. One example of first name being important is the relationship with Paul and Barnabas. In the beginning, Barnabas was the leader of the group, his name coming before Paul's (a.k.a. Saul). With time, Paul became the leader of the team and his name always preceded that of Barnabas.

5. Like many Pentecostal preacher women in history, Priscilla was probably a woman with a calling to do a great work for the Lord and her husband was the strong supporter who stayed out of the limelight. Much should be said for Aquila and any other man who is willing to stand in his wife's shadow. But this did not make Priscilla insubordinate or better than her man. As a wife she could be a submissive and sup-

portive partner, but she also had an obligation to respond to the call of God on her life, whatever that involved.

6. Priscilla and Aquila taught or "expounded" (*exethento*) spiritual truths just as Paul expounded (*exetitheto*).
7. Bailey, *Paul Through Mediterranean Eyes*, 412.
8. Belleville, *Women Leaders and the Church*, 165.
9. David M. Scholer, "I Timothy 2:9–15 & the place of women in the church's ministry," *Women, Authority & the Bible*, Alvera Mickelsen, ed. (Downers Grove, IL: InterVarsity, 1986), 199.
10. In I Timothy 1:3, this is the gender inclusive pronoun *tis* and in II Timothy 2:2 the "faithful *men*" is *anthrōpois* which refers to *persons* not just the male gender.
11. Trombley, *Who Said Women Can't Teach?*, 34; *Babylonian Talmud, Kiddushin*, 70a.
12. Staton, *The Biblical Liberation of Women*, 128. See Matthew 28:5–7; John 4:19–26, 28–30, 39; II Timothy 2:1–2.
13. Some opponents of women in ministry like Wayne Grudem and John Piper have opposed the idea of women being taught theology and pastoral ministry in Bible schools.
14. From the Greek *sigaō*.
15. From the Greek *hēsuchia* or *hēsychia*. This word is different from the one used in I Corinthians 14:34–35. The silence called for in Corinth was *sigaō*, a silencing of the spoken word. The silence involved in Ephesus was *hēsychia*, a word not nearly so severe. This *hēsychia* appears in Acts 22:2 where the riotous crowd quieted down and respectfully listened to Paul. Seeing that the Ephesian believers were in a riot of a sort, it would make sense for Paul to call for calmness, especially if wives were the cause. No doubt, not all believers are called to voicelessness but all are to exercise humility and restraint.
16. II Thessalonians 3:11–12.
17. Perhaps translators assumed that women need to be silenced while men only need quietness, reflecting some mild gender bias in their translation of certain words. It would make more sense when one reads this letter about the disruption of false doctrine in the church, that not only the men needed to calm down (to be "without wrath" in verse 8) but also the women needed to learn some "quietness."
18. In I Timothy 2:2, the word "peaceable" is from *hēsuchios*, and *hēsuchia* for "silence" or "calmness" in 2:11–12. Knofel Staton, *The Biblical Liberation of Women for Leadership in the Church* (Eugene, OR: Wipf and Stock, 2003), 129, says, "The Greek word *escuchios* in v.2 (quiet) and *esuchia* in v.11 (quietness) are twin words that appear in only four other texts in the New Testament, none of which refers to being verbally muzzled. In other texts, the same word used in verse 11 described someone having a peaceful, settled down, calmed down, contemplative, and sweet disposition." Also n. 135 says "2 Thessalonians 3:12; Titus 2:2; 1 Peter 3:4, and Acts 22:2." While Acts 22:2 might give the impression that perfect silence is in view, the context is one of an uproar and mob action in Acts 21:33–35. The need in Ephesus was to calm tensions, too.
19. Keener, *Paul*, 101.
20. Reformed (Calvinist) theologian Grudem rejects such notions in *Evangelical Feminism: a New Path to Liberalism?* (Wheaton, Ill: Crossway, 2006), 104: "Can a pastor or the elders of a church give a woman permission to disobey this statement of Scripture? Certainly not! Can a woman do what the Bible says not to do and excuse it by saying, 'I'm under the authority of the elders'? Would we say that the elders of a church could tell people 'under their authority' that they have permission to disobey other passages of Scripture?" Truly, I Timothy 2:12 does not say she cannot teach a man "unless her husband is present." If a husband can give his wife the right to violate scripture, then how many other verses could they agree to discard? Lying? Theft? Ananias tried that with Sapphira and God struck them dead. No, such a "pastor or husband must approve" teaching is unsupported by this passage under discussion. Notice that this verse says nothing about her being a "pastor," it never says "if she stays submitted," and it says nothing about "being in charge" of something. Should a female minister be submitted

to her leadership? Of course! So should a male minister. This verse, however, does not deal with that subject.
21. How far does such thinking go? Can a mother not speak into the life of a grown son? Can she only teach him until he is 13, or 15, or 18? Would it be wrong for my mother to teach me something now? Of course, Paul would frown at such a discussion because these concepts were nowhere near what he was speaking to when he wrote these letters.
22. We find many biblical mentions of woman leaders in contrast with a passage some have taken to mean women cannot lead. The evangelical interpretation of scripture would say one would have to obey the teaching of the epistles rather than the stories one might find in the narratives of Scripture (i.e., salvation proof text from Romans rather than from the accounts in Acts). The key Pentecostal argument for speaking in tongues being the evidence of the Spirit baptism comes from the multiple narrative mentions in Acts, not the epistles. To be consistent then, Bible believers should value the narrative evidence of women in ministry over one passage which some have perceived to be in opposition. In his paper "Exploring the Glass Ceiling: Women Who Minister" (Urshan Graduate School of Theology Symposium 2003), 2, David Norris says "Indeed, we even go so far as to say that tongues are the initial evidence of the baptism of the Holy Ghost and baptism in Jesus name is normative because we see the repetition of this pattern in the biblical narrative. If then we are to be consistent in our hermeneutic, there can be no question: women can and do minister."
23. Grudem, *Evangelical Feminism & Biblical Truth*, 180, references Cranfield, *Critical and Exegetical Commentary on the Epistle to the Romans*, 1979 2:784, which says Pricilla's prominence indicates she was either the more outgoing person in the marriage, she was more well-known, or she was of wealthy and noble birth.
24. Supposing Andronicus is Junia's husband and not brother, another possibility.
25. I Corinthians 7:26, 32–34; I Timothy 5:5. Paul most likely meant for this recommendation to apply only on account of a contemporary "distress" and not a ruling for all time.
26. Acts 12:12; 16:40; 1:11; I Corinthians 16:15, 17; Colossians 4:15; Philemon 1–2. Aida B. Spencer, *Beyond the Curse: Women Called to Ministry* (Peabody, MA: Hendrickson, 1985), 119, references the idea that there is a possible mention of another woman leader named Stephana, although this is presented as male "Stephanas" in most translations.
27. Paul spoke directly to the false teaching problems that both his apostle-trainees were to address but did not ever say women were to blame (II Timothy 2:16, 25–26; 3:5; Titus 1:10–11; 3:10–11). I. Howard Marshall, "Women in Ministry: A Further Look at I Timothy 2," *Women, Ministry and the Gospel*, Husbands and Larsen, eds., 70.
28. II Timothy 2:2 says "And the things that you have heard from me. . . commit these to faithful [persons (*anthrōpos*)] who will be able to teach others also."
29. I Corinthians 12:8–10; 14:6, 26; Colossians 3:16.
30. See Acts 13:1; 18:25–26; 28:23; Romans 2:18; I Corinthians 14:19, 26; Galatians 6:6; Colossians 3:16; I Timothy 4:13; Titus 2:3; I Timothy 3:2 and the parallel uses of *didaskō* and *katēcheō*, and *ektithēmi*. Also, the gift of teaching connects with the gift of "shepherding" as "pastor-teacher" in Ephesians 4:11. Teaching is also what those who prophesy do (*katecheo* 'to instruct') in I Corinthians 14:19.
31. The word for co-workers is *synergos* in Romans 16:3, 9, 21; I Corinthians 3:9; II Corinthians 1:24; 8:23; I Thessalonians 3:2; Philippians 2:25; Philemon 24. He does not use "co-workers" to describe Christians in general.
32. Witherington, *Women*, 183.
33. Ibid. See Acts 18; Romans 16; I Corinthians 4:17; 16:10; I Thessalonians 1:1; 3:2, 6.
34. Spencer, *Beyond the Curse*, 119. Spencer gives author's translation of Philippians 4:2. *Sunathleō* can be translated in this way if context allows it. Paul puts these two women on the level of Clement, which would suggest they helped plant churches.
35. Witherington, *Women*, 186.
36. Romans 16:3–4.
37. Romans 16:7.
38. Romans 16:6, 12. Paul uses the verb *kopiao*, which means to 'work hard.'

39. Witherington and Hyatt, *Paul's Letter to the Romans*, 387, n. 48.
40. Keener, "Women," 215.
41. This command comes in I Corinthians 16:16, right after the discussion of the household of Stephanas. If this really was Stephana (see note 26, above), Paul gave direct commands for the church to submit to a woman leader of a congregation.
42. Wilshire, *Insight into Two Biblical Passages*, 40–41.

CHAPTER 6
HE CALLED SARAH: WOMEN AS DAUGHTERS

1. The battleground passages for women in ministry cause people of all denominational and doctrinal persuasions to discuss key verses that teach modesty in adornment, long hair, and speaking in tongues—things many groups do not uphold. One big difference between the holiness Pentecostal understanding of these scriptures and the evangelical way of looking at them is that we believe these passages on modesty apply to us today. Many evangelicals explain such passages away, saying it was just a cultural thing, but then some of them turn and say the "women in silence" passages must be enforced!
2. Kenter Doje and Stanley Scism, *Little Lady* (Bridgeton, MO: Wonderful Words, 1990), 36–38.
3. As reflected in many other translations. The word *dialogismos* can refer to both internal conflict (doubting, double-mindedness) and external conflict with another, as in, "Do all things without complaining and *disputing*." (Philippians 2:14, emphasis added).
4. Doug Ellingsworth, *Call Me Blessed* (Dyersburg, TN: Seven Orders, 2015), 54, quoting *Vanity Fair*, May 2001.
5. Ibid., 55.
6. Traditionally, married Jewish women wore their hair up.
7. J. P. V. D. Balsdon, *Roman Women: Their History and Habits* (London: Bodley Head, 1962), 256.
8. Ibid., 258.
9. Ibid., 263.
10. Ibid., 264.
11. In workplaces and schools, females face overwhelming pressure to conform to current trends in hairstyles, accessories, and clothing. When a woman comes to the Lord and discovers His heart for modesty, she is freed from being a slave to the expectation to conform to many such societal expectations.
12. Rebecca Mendizabal Johnson, personal communication, March 3, 2016.
13. This does not apply only to wives, of course, because all sweet-spirited women, whether single, married, or widowed, make the church beautiful.
14. Staton, *The Biblical Liberation of Women*, 124. Over the centuries since the reformation, Luther, Estius, Calovius, Matthies, Garrett, Erdman, Burn, Gouge, Williams, and C. K. Barrett are theologians and commentators who have noted that I Timothy 2:11–12 regards wives' behavior.
15. This religion threatened males in a very personal way: male cultic priests were castrated.
16. Mary said she had not slept with "a man" which we translate correctly as "husband" (Luke 1:34). Anna lived with "a man" meaning "husband" for seven years (Luke 2:36). Jesus did not use a possessive pronoun (like "her husband") when He mentioned divorcing "a man," but this could only have meant "husband" (Luke 16:18). Paul said, "A wife is not to depart from her husband" saying literally "a woman is not to depart from a man" (I Corinthians 7:10). Those instances illustrate that one does not need a pronoun or article to make either word mean "spouse" (From *gunē*, "woman" and *anēr*, "man."). Furthermore, if Paul meant males or females generically, he had other ways of saying so. See the discussion in Gordon P. Hugenberger,

"Women in Church Office: Hermeneutics or Exegesis? A Survey of Approaches to I Tim 2:8–15," *JETS*, 35/3, Sept 1992, 353–54.

17. Fredrick J. Long, "Christ's Gifted Bride: Gendered Members in Ministry in Acts and Paul," *Women, Ministry and the Gospel*, Husbands and Larsen, eds., 99, n. 6.
18. In the two phrases "I exhort first of all that supplications, prayers, intercessions, and giving of thanks be made for all men" and "there is one God and one Mediator between God and men," Paul chose a word for "men" in general which can be translated as 'mankind' or 'humanity.' Then, he becomes gender specific with his remarks in verse 8 using the word for men that refers to males specifically. Staton, 122, says, "Each New Testament writer shifted from *anthropos* to *aner* when the topic shifted from the male gender (or generic people) to husbands." After 2:1 and 2:5, "Paul shifted from men (males or generic people) to husbands specifically by shifting from *anthropos* to *aner* in 2:8 and 2:12."
19. First Timothy 2:9–15 parallels other Scriptures addressing husbands and wives. References to Adam and Eve in verses 13–14 parallel what Paul wrote in an earlier letter regarding husbands and wives referencing the first couple (Ephesians 5:22–33). Textual indicators bracket verses 9–15 as one unit, not as a random list of comments. Therefore, since the reference to childbearing in verse 15 is indisputably pertaining to a wife, the whole passage speaks first to married woman.
20. Gordon P. Hugenberger, "Women in Church Office: Hermeneutics or Exegesis? A Survey of Approaches to 1 Tim 2:8-15," *JETS*, 35/3, Sept 1992: 341–60, 350–51.
21. Staton, *The Biblical Liberation of Women*, 123. While not every word is the same in the original, the themes and topics are. Several Greek words are identical in both pericopes: "*proseuche, andros, gune, esuchia, kosmos, chrusios, imation, theos.*"
22. Hugenberger, "Women in Church Office," 356–57.
23. Staton, *The Biblical Liberation of Women*, 128, says, "Paul masterfully bracketed the wife's relationship with her husband by the same Greek word, *sophrosunes* (propriety) at the beginning (9) and at the ending (15) of this section. Placing that word at both ends characterizes the entirety of 9–15, which focuses more upon the interior character of the woman than upon exterior decorum and speech. The wife [should] frame her communication with her character not clothing, patience not pearls, helpfulness not hair[styles], inner disposition not outer decorum."
24. I Timothy 2:11–12, NIV (2011). The italicized words come from the NIV footnotes.
25. "But I permit not a woman to teach, nor to have dominion over a man," I Timothy 2:12 ASV. Similarly constructed sentences in the New Testament justify reading this phrase as: "I do not permit a wife to teach in order to gain mastery over a husband." For example, Matthew 6:26 could read: "thief breaks in *in order to* steal," Matt. 13:13 could read: "they do not hear *so that* they do not understand," and Acts 17:24 could read "God does not live in temples *in order to* be served by human hands." This shows one of six ways the "*ouk . . . oude*" grammatical construction could be read. The strength of the discussion does not lean on this translation, but given the content of the passage, the words move from general to more specific: "teach" (general) to "*authenteō*" (more specific). Clearly, Paul was not opposing all female teaching but a specific teaching that intended to demean or destroy the male roles.
26. This interpretation comes from the Greek word *authenteō*, the meaning of which is disputed. Some linguists and scholars argue that in the context of I Timothy 2:12, this word does not mean "to take authority" but instead means "to murder" or "to instigate violence." See a thorough discussion about the scholarship surrounding this debate in my master's thesis, "Putting a Woman in Her Place: Females as Biblical Teachers, Elders, and Pastors" (Urshan Graduate School of Theology, 2014).
27. Genesis 21:12.
28. The construction of this phrase in verse 12 is an "either/or" or "neither/nor" construction. Some scholars argue that since the second verb is clearly negative (originally "to do violence," as Wilshire defends, or "usurp authority") then the word "teach" must also have a negative connotation in this context. The secondary verb of violence or usurping authority then must be the content of the referenced teaching. In other words, she is not to do teaching that leads to destruction of the husband or his role in the home. See Belleville, "Women," *Two Views*, 88. Also see Belleville, *Leaders*, 176–77.

29. I Timothy 1:4; 4:1; 5:15; Titus 3:9.
30. Zens, *What's with Paul and Women?*, 92.
31. Acts 19:34.
32. Belleville, *Leaders*, 177.
33. I Corinthians 15:32.
34. Zens, *What's with Paul and Women?*, 92, emphasis mine. Acts 19:21–41 tells the story of Paul surviving the riot in Ephesus.
35. Acts 19:23-41 describes this riot.
36. I Timothy 2:11, author's translation.
37. Many times God privileged the second one to rule over the first, as with Jacob and Esau, Isaac and Ishmael, and the Second Adam over the Adam in Eden. Also, in Paul's use of "first, then" syntax the dead are not better than the living believers in I Thessalonians 4:16–17 but follow sequential order. This *"prōtos... eita"* construct does little more than show a sequence of ideas. See Mark 4:28; I Corinthians 15:46; I Timothy 3:10; James 3:17.
38. Zens, *What's with Paul and Women?*, 94.
39. Richard C. and Catherine C Kroeger, *I Suffer Not a Woman: Rethinking 1 Timothy 2:11–15 in Light of Ancient Evidence* (Grand Rapids, MI: Baker, 1992), 105–13.
40. Belleville, *Leaders*, 178. Much debate surrounds the timing for a full-orbed Gnostic belief system. However, early hints of this movement's beginning can be seen even in the first century. Much of what the Apostle John fought in his epistles appears to be a proto-Gnostic heresy as well.
41. Romans 5:12–19.
42. Andrew Perriman, *Speaking of Women* (Leicester, England: Apollos, 1998), 161.
43. Keener, *Paul*, 117.
44. I Timothy 1:19–20.
45. Actually "males" from *anēr* in Acts 20:29–30.
46. Marshall, *Women, Ministry and the Gospel*, Husbands and Larsen, eds., 70, referencing Wayne Grudem's perspectives on women, a view Marshall does not hold.
47. Ibid., 65.
48. Titus 2:4.
49. Mary Hayter, The New Eve in Christ: *The Use and Abuse of the Bible in the Debate about Women in the Church* (Grand Rapids, MI: Eerdmans, 1987), 141. See II Corinthians 11:3.
50. II Corinthians 11:13–15.
51. Keener, *Paul*, 114, 129, n. 106–09. Hayter, *The New Eve in Christ,* 141. Kroeger and Kroeger, in *I Suffer Not a Woman* go into great detail describing not only the Ephesian traditions regarding women, but also the proto-gnostic heresies regarding Eve. These stories may or may not have been prominent in Ephesus, but are very telling in that they describe Eve as being created first, forming Adam, being enlightened by the serpent, and/or giving wisdom to Adam. Though Gnosticism had many varied forms, it specialized in upending traditional teachings. In one myth, God became their evil force, the serpent the positive force, and so on. It would not be a surprise to see many of these "preeminent Eve" stories thriving in female-centric Ephesus where Artemis provided a similar influence. If so, then the Jewish fables and pagan myths may have collided in one ideology Paul had to address. See I Timothy 1:4; 4:7; II Timothy 2:16; 4:4. Especially interesting is his command to Timothy about "avoiding the profane and idle babblings and contradictions of what is falsely called knowledge [*gnōsis*]" I Timothy 6:20.
52. Spencer, *Beyond the Curse*, 91.
53. Craig L. Blomberg, "Women in Ministry: A Complementarian Perspective," *Two Views*, 172.
54. Belleville, "Women in Ministry: An Egalitarian Perspective," *Two Views*, 91.
55. Zens, *What's with Paul and Women?*, 93.

56. For example, the rich young ruler in Matthew was told to give away all that he had. Does this mean everyone should give up everything they own to be saved? No. It means those whose hearts are trapped with a love of money need to give without reserve and free their souls up for salvation. The same principle applies to those who are in love with a hobby that takes away from the focus they should have on the Lord, working for His kingdom, and meeting the needs of their families.

57. E. Earle Ellis, Pauline Theology: *Ministry and Society* (Grand Rapids, MI: Eerdmans, 1989), 74.

CHAPTER 7
HE CALLED ESTHER: WOMEN IN AUTHORITY

1. Esther 4:14.
2. Belleville, "Women," *Two Views*, 83. The disputed word is *authentein*. I engage this complex discussion and the scholarship surrounding this word in my thesis *Putting a Woman in Her Place*.
3. Greek *exousia*. Matthew 8:8–9. The centurion understood Jesus' authority to command disease in the same way he issued orders to his soldiers who had to obey because of the imperial authority he was under.
4. Belleville, "Women," *Two Views*, 65. Matthew 21:23.
5. Acts 8:19.
6. Acts 9:14; 26:10.
7. Luke 4:6.
8. Walter Liefeld, "A Plural Ministry View," *Women in Ministry: Four Views*, Bonnidell Clouse and Robert C. Clouse, eds. (Downers Grove, IL: InterVarsity, 1989), 258.
9. II Corinthians 1:24.
10. Hebrews 13:7.
11. Belleville, "Women," *Two Views*, 102.
12. Revelation 2:20–23.
13. Notice that there was another church with a different issue: the spirit of Balaam (Revelation 2:14). This had nothing to do with gender.
14. If you are dealing with such a spirit, prayer is the key. Deep, intercessory prayer has broken this spirit when it manifested against me in times past. My wife and I have seen this spirit stopped quickly by agreeing together and binding it so it cannot do its work. In its place, prayer warriors should loose the spirit of humility and submission. See Matthew 16:19; 18:18–20; Ephesians 6:12. A good resource on this topic is the video series "Overcoming the Spirit of Jezebel" by Jason Sciscoe.
15. Acts 9:26, 30–31. The churches then had rest (peace) possibly because the stress of dealing with Paul had ended!
16. Ashley Stewart, "Young Women in Ministry," *Pentecostal Herald*, July 2012, 28.
17. Frank J. Ewart, *The Phenomenon of Pentecost*, revised (Hazelwood, MO: Word Aflame, 2000), 15–16.
18. Spiritual authority flows in the lives of those who are in submission. A military man realized this principle at work in Jesus' ministry. He said, "I also am a man placed under authority, having soldiers under me. And I say to one, 'Go,' and he goes; and to another, 'Come,' and he comes; and to my servant, 'Do this,' and he does it." (Luke 7:8). The servants did not obey him because of who he was but because of the authority he was under: the Emperor's. To have spiritual authority, a child of God must be submitted to His leaders.
19. There are biblical instances when God's ministers brought judgment down on those who opposed them. This does not mean one held control over others but that those who opposed were rebelling against God. For example, when Paul struck Elymas blind it was not because of personal reasons; Elymas was opposing Paul's message and trying to turn someone away from the faith. When people were cast out of a church, as the New Testament records, it was because they opposed God, not an individual. Notice that Paul calls the whole church to cast out the sinning brother

in I Corinthians 5 because the church as a body has the authority of God, not just a single person.
20. Lucile Farmer, "The Story of Lucile Farmer," *Profiles of Pentecostal Missionaries*, Mary Wallace, ed. (Hazelwood, MO: Word Aflame, 1986), 65–66.
21. II Corinthians 6:1–13; Ephesians 3:1; 4:1.
22. Susan T. Foh, "A Male Leadership View: The Head of the Woman Is the Man," *Women in Ministry*, Bonnidell Clouse and Robert C. Clouse, eds.
23. I Thessalonians 5:12–13.

CHAPTER 8

HE CALLED PHOEBE: WOMEN AS MINISTERS

1. Robert Jewett, "Paul, Phoebe, and the Spanish Mission," *The Social World of Formative Christianity and Judaism*, Jacob Neusner, et al., eds. (Philadelphia, PA: Fortress, 1988), 148–53.
2. Grudem, *Evangelical Feminism & Biblical Truth*, 222, using definitions from BDAG and Louw-Nida, says the word *prostatis* for a woman puts her in a supportive role, like a patron, benefactor, guardian, protectress, or patroness.
3. See especially I Thessalonians 5:12 and I Timothy 5:17. The word also shows up in Romans 12:8; I Timothy 3:4–5, 12; Titus 3:8, 14; and Luke 10:34–35. Foh, *Women in Ministry*, 78.
4. Romans 12:8.
5. Witherington and Hyatt, *Paul's Letter to the Romans*, 384–85.
6. Acts 12:12; 16:14–15; Romans 16:1–2; Colossians 4:15.
7. Jewett, "Paul, Phoebe," 149.
8. Luke T. Johnson, *Reading Romans: A Literary and Theological Commentary* (New York: Crossroad, 1997), 7.
9. Ephesians 6:21–22; Philippians 2:25–30; Colossians 4:7–9.
10. Keener, *Paul*, 238. In Romans 16, Paul mentions several women in ministry. If he had not meant us to understand that they were preachers, teachers, and leaders in the church, he would have put a disclaimer here. This list of women appears in a separate book from those epistles that have apparent prohibitions against women preachers. Paul wrote to Rome, covering important details of doctrine for a church where he had never been. He certainly would not have been so forgetful to not include a disclaimer against women preachers after leaving the impression they were a good thing. In fact, if Paul had a doctrine against women in ministry, it was another huge oversight on his part to send a woman to present his letter!
11. Romans 15:8; I Corinthians 3:5.
12. Deacon, minister, and servant come from *diakonos*.
13. Witherington, *Romans*, 382, emphasis original. Witherington recommends (in n. 27), Wright, "Romans," 762. Wright says, "It is interesting, however, that Origen takes this passage to indicate that women were ordained in the church's ministry by apostolic authority. Pelagius in his commentary on Romans indicates that in his day [in the fourth and fifth centuries] women were allowed to baptized other women and preach the word to them." See G. Bray, ed., *Romans: Ancient Christian Commentary on Scripture*, Downers Grove: InterVaristy, 1998)," 369. K. Romaniuk, "Was Phoebe in Romans 16:1 a Deaconess?"
14. Bailey, *Paul Through Mediterranean Eyes*, 411.
15. F. F. Bruce, *Commentary on the Book of Acts*, NICNT (Grand Rapids, MI: Eerdmans, 1977), 130, says the best rendering of *diakonos* is probably "minister."
16. Mark 10:45 uses the verbal form of deacon, *diakoneō*.
17. Although they are not called "deacons" (*diakonos*) in Acts 6:1–7, the verb used to describe their actions is *diakoneō*.
18. Oddly enough, many church groups use the title "deacons" for the board of directors who oversee the pastor, even hiring and firing him. This is a reversal of the first-century order where bishops oversaw and appointed deacons.

19. Romans 15:9; I Corinthians 3:5; II Corinthians 3:6; 6:4; II Corinthians 11:23; Ephesians 3:7; 6:21; Colossians 1:7, 23, 25; 4:7.
20. Paul blurred the lines in his use of the term when "he applies it most commonly to ministers of the gospel." Keener, *Paul*, 239.
21. Woman or wife is *gunē*. I find it troubling that some translators have no qualms about using the word "wife" here yet do not use "wife" or "husband" in I Timothy 2:11–12 where the context is clearly about spouses.
22. Belleville, *Women*, 62.
23. This would then read, "Likewise ministers… Likewise women… Let the ministers," addressing expectations for female ministers who are not distinct from but distinct within the minister grouping. Joh. Ed. Huther, *Critical and Exegetical Hand-Book to the Epistles to Timothy and Titus*, Trans. from 4th edition of German by David Hunter (New York: Funk & Wagnalls, 1885), 124–25.
24. I John 2:13–14. John refers to the local leaders as "fathers" and the new believers as "little children" much the way Jesus did.
25. Titus 2:4–5, 6–8. Similar to how he addressed bishops and then deacons in I Timothy 3, Paul here addresses the elders and then the youngers.
26. These ministers served in various capacities as already mentioned, but a bishop would have been one who oversaw other such servants in the kingdom.
27. Belleville, "Women," 63.
28. I Timothy 5:9. Just as he expects a church leader to be maritally faithful, so he expected a widow to have been faithful in her marriage: "*mias gynaikos andra* (3:2, 12) and *henos andros gynē* (5:9)" essentially "a one-woman man" and "a one-man woman." Obviously marital faithfulness was expected of both genders and especially of those in leadership roles. The widow was a leader even if she was not an outspoken one. She gave herself to prayer and if nothing else taught the younger women how to be good wives and mothers in Titus 2:3–5.
29. Acts 6:1–5 with 8:5–13.
30. Joan Morris, *The Lady Was a Bishop* (New York: Macmillan, 1973), 6–7. Pliny called them *ministrae*, in an official communication, and considered them leaders of the services.
31. Witherington, *Romans*, 382, in n. 27, quoting Wright, "Romans," 762.
32. Matthew 28:19.
33. Kathy White, "Opal Jones Blackford," *Pioneer Pentecostal Women*, Vol. 1, Mary H. Wallace, ed. (Hazelwood, MO: Word Aflame, 1981), 14–15.
34. Marshall, "Women in Ministry," *Women, Ministry and the Gospel*, Husbands and Larsen, eds., 63.
35. Russell C. Prohl, *Woman in the Church: A Restudy of Woman's Place in Building the Kingdom* (Grand Rapids, MI: Eerdmans, 1957), 79.
36. Spencer, *Beyond the Curse*, 113.
37. Wilshire, *Insight into Two Biblical Passages*, 52.
38. Belleville, *Women*, 61–62.
39. The Pentecostal movement embraces people of all races and involves both genders equally in ministry because of the unifying Spirit of God. The spirit of gender-confusion is not part of that unifying Spirit. We must not blur the lines but stay strong in holiness. If we leave behind our practices of being separate from the world and distinct in gender, we will also lose the blessing of Pentecost. Holiness Pentecost remains distinct from other spiritual movements because of this consecration. We can win the battle against wickedness as we create a climate where revival can be birthed.
40. Lindley, *You Have Stept Out of Your Place*, 118.
41. Ibid., 119–20. She defended her ministry in *The Promise of the Father* and influenced thousands through a later book *The Way of Holiness* and a periodical *The Guide to Holiness*.
42. Ibid., 121.
43. John 4:36; I Corinthians 3:5–8.

44. There are gender distinctive terms that do not seem to patronize as much, however. Gender distinctive terms such as *Lord* and *Lady* or *Sir* and *Ma'am* seem to be on par with each other, although still carrying a cultural stigma. In the church, *Brother* and *Sister* are parallel terms unless someone's own misogynist perspective has redefined the terms.
45. Acts 15:38–39. Jewett, "Paul, Phoebe," 148–53.

CHAPTER 9

HE CALLED LYDIA: WOMEN AS PASTORS

1. Philippians 3:2–3.
2. Chris Anderson, "Eva Hunt: Pioneer of Home Missions," Unpublished paper written for Urshan Graduate School of Theology, Apr 2003: 5, accessed July 1, 2014, referencing a private interview with Pastor Thomas Suey of Herrick, IL, pastor of a church founded by Eva Hunt.
3. Lindley, *You Have Stept Out of Your Place*, 336–37.
4. Norris, "Glass Ceiling," 11.
5. Lindley, *You Have Stept Out of Your Place*, 335–36.
6. Ibid., 334.
7. Felicity Dale, "What Dr. Cho Taught Me about Women in Revival," July 23, 2013, accessed February 3, 2014, http://www.charismamag.com/life/women/18328-what-dr-cho-taught-me-about-women-in-revival
8. Shepherd/pastor (*poimainō*), leader/guide (*proistēmi*), overseer/bishop (*episkopos*), elder/presbyter (*presbyteros*), and deacon/servant/minister (*diakonos*). In the phrase "he who leads, with diligence" in Romans 12:8, the underlying Greek word for *he* is a gender neutral pronoun and the word *leads* is *proistēmi*.
9. Acts 20:17.
10. Acts 20:28.
11. I Peter 5:2.
12. Keener, *Women*, 210.
13. Acts 13:1.
14. In the KJV and NKJV, only one Scripture uses the general term pastor (Ephesians 4:11), but individuals were typically called elders or by their function in the church as in prophet, teacher, and so on.
15. From a gender neutral pronoun *ei tis*, in I Timothy 3:1, meaning "whoever" or "anyone."
16. The word *episkopeō* here shares the same root as "bishop" or "overseer."
17. Matthew 25:43, key word here: *episkeptomai*.
18. I Timothy 3:4–5. Walter Liefeld, "A Plural Ministry View," *Women in Ministry: Four Views*, Bonnidell Clouse and Robert C. Clouse, eds. (Downers Grove, I: InterVarsity, 1989), 147, says, "It is striking that when Paul lists the qualifications for elders, his reason for mentioning the importance of ruling one's family well is not so the elder can 'rule' the church, but rather so he can 'care' (*epimeleomai*) for it".
19. Deuteronomy 24:1–4.
20. Mark 10:12. Of course, He taught against the idea of either gender divorcing his or her spouse.
21. Matthew 19:11–12.
22. Keener, *Paul*, 110.
23. Matthew 23:23–24; Mark 10:5–9.
24. David K. Bernard, *Spiritual Leadership in the Twenty-first Century: Advice for Ministers and Church Leaders* (Hazelwood, MO: Word Aflame, 2015), 28–29.
25. Matthew 7:15–20.
26. Belleville, "A Response to Thomas Schreiner," 325, in *Two Views*, ed. Beck.

27. Rufina of Smyrna, Peristeria of Thebes in Thessaly, Theopempte of Myndos (near Ephesus), and Sophia of Gortyn on Crete were female, synagogue rulers we have discovered from history. Belleville, *Leaders*, 24.
28. See Luke 13:14; Acts 13:15.
29. Witherington, *Women*, 189, says, "We noted earlier that in traditional Roman religion women did not have such a variety of roles, and it is not surprising that Christianity was affecting a considerable number of Roman women and giving them active roles to play." Of course, this climate was different from female-goddess-laden Ephesus.
30. Acts 12:12.
31. The Greek term for "shepherd" (*poimēn*) closely parallels the word for "feeding" (*poimainō*). Some would argue that a better meaning is that one "shepherd" the sheep, which would involve more than just feeding. Of course, the answer in both definitions is yes, a woman can do that.
32. In I Timothy 4:14, Timothy had received an anointing through the elders, yet he now transfers such a blessing appointing other elders.
33. I Peter 5:2, and must be careful not to serve "for dishonest gain." Also, I Timothy 5:18 indicates that they were paid.
34. James 5:14.
35. John 21:15-17; II Timothy 4:2.
36. I Timothy 5:19–20.
37. The prophecy by Paul in Acts 20:30 says "men" (from *anēr*) will arise and lead some astray. These are probably Hymenaeus and Alexander whom he later mentions in I Timothy 1:20.
38. The enigmatic "woman not to teach" passage is in I Timothy 2:12 whereas it is men who are deceiving gullible women in II Timothy 3:6.
39. As they did in all the churches: Acts 14:23. See Liefeld, "A Plural Ministry View," 266.
40. Paul first speaks of elders (*presbuteros*) in Titus 1:5 and then refers to *presbutēs* (elderly man) and *presbutis* (elderly woman) in Titus 2:23.
41. Huther, 306, says, "These facts tend to show how completely the Apostle's mind, in all the suggestions as to the officials of the church, or those in any more public station among the body of believers, was upon the moral and Christian qualifications which were needed, and how very slight, as yet, was the development of the idea of government, authority or office in the churches." T. Scott Womble, *Beyond Reasonable Doubt: 95 Theses which Dispute the Church's Conviction Against Women* (Xulon, 2008), 136, says, "While this is the only occurrence of *presbuteras* in the Bible, it is clear that it is the feminine form of the Greek word for elder (*presbuteros*)."
42. I Timothy 5:1–2; Titus 2:4–5, 6-8; I John 2:13–14 in concert with I Timothy 3:9–12.
43. "Old wives" *graōdēs*.
44. The New Testament indicates that each church had multiple elders, not just one. These pastors would most likely all relate to one leader such as Timothy or Paul but lead in concert on the local scene. Such leadership would likely have included the ministry gifts of both males and females. While this form is not intentionally followed in much of Pentecost, the idea of various ministry gifts and skills contributing to the local church is vital, no matter the personal labels applied. Keener says these "pastors, who were probably teams of supervising members within house churches, were not the 'highest' office. . . we do have examples of women exercising 'higher' authority than this." ("A response to Craig Blomberg," 187).
45. See also I Timothy 3:2.
46. Spencer, *Beyond the Curse*, 110, says, "A church would have to be called *either* elect lady *or* children in John's language scheme, not both." Emphasis original.
47. Ibid., 111. The term *elect* can refer to someone chosen for ministry, such as Rufus in Romans 16:13 and in other first-century documents.
48. Ibid., 109. To complement the masculine *kurios* (master) in Greek, we find *kuria* (lady) used of the opposite gender. Hence, *kuria* is the feminine form of the word "lord" or an esteemed person.

49. I Timothy 5:1–2. This passage "can be translated 'Do not rebuke *an elder [presbuteros]* but exhort him as you would a father; treat younger men like brothers, *women elders [presbuteras]* like mothers, younger women like sisters, in all purity.'" Bailey, 411–12, emphasis original. Could he just be referring to older women and older men? Possibly. However, he says all this in the context of talking about how to treat the exemplary widows (devoted female role-models) which closes by speaking about pastors in general (5:17–19).
50. John 13:5, 14–15; I Peter 2:21.
51. Sarah Sumner, *Men and Women in the Church* (Downers Grove, IL: InterVarsity, 2003), 214.
52. Matthew 23:6–12.

CHAPTER 10
HE CALLED EVE: WOMEN AS LADIES

1. Genesis 1:27–28, says, "Then God blessed *them*, and God said to *them*. . ." emphasis added.
2. Nona Freeman, *A Prophet in Our Time* (Minden, LA: Barnes, 2007), 85.
3. Thomas R. Schreiner, "Women in Ministry: A Complementarian Perspective," 315, in *Two Views*, ed. Beck.
4. Romans 5:12, 14.
5. Since Genesis chapter 2 is a more detailed explanation of 1:26–30, the statement in 2:18 precedes the declaration in 1:31.
6. Hayter, *The New Eve in Christ,* 120, says the idea "of a descending hierarchical order is weakened once it is acknowledged that *kaphale* was used to signify 'source' and not 'superior rank' in pre-biblical Greek." Grudem, *Evangelical Feminism and Biblical Truth*, 203–04, challenges the "*kephalē* means source" hypothesis and suggests that some contemporary Greek uses of the word would have been interpreted as "beginning." Grudem, however, does not believe in women in leadership.
7. Christ was not physically present until His birth in Bethlehem. He was the pattern, so to speak, by which man was formed.
8. Daniel J. Koren, *Double Identity* (Neosho, MO: Living Springs, 2007) 108–10.
9. Men and women must keep gender distinctions from one another regarding hair in honor of their source or in recognition of their point of beginning. They do not make a decision about their physical image themselves because they did not begin with themselves.
10. I Corinthians 11:15.
11. Hebrews 1:3.
12. Hayter, *The New Eve in Christ,* 120.
13. Of course, many other passages in Scripture show how gender distinctions matter in the home and must be maintained in social roles. Spiritually, however, men have no greater authority than women in the church body because any power we have comes through Jesus Christ. More on this in the chapter, "He Called Ruth."
14. Conservative patriarchy and family movements (including Bill Gothard seminars) have seemed to push a philosophy that every wife and daughter's decisions must go through the man of the house.
15. Katharine C. Bushnell, *God's Word to Women* (Minneapolis, MN: Christians for Biblical Equality, 2003), 100. Emphasis removed.
16. Olive Haney, "Frank and Elizabeth May Gray," *Profiles of Pentecostal Missionaries*, Mary Wallace, ed. (Hazelwood, MO: Word Aflame, 1986), 878–8.
17. Schreiner, "Women in Ministry," 318, in *Two Views*, ed. Beck.
18. Witherington, *Women*, 169.
19. The NKJV unfortunately adds the italicized words "*a symbol of*" in assuming that the covering on the woman's head is merely symbolic. These words are italicized to show that they were not in the original text and were supplied by translators to

(hopefully) clarify the passage; therefore, by removing that phrase in the quote we are in harmony with the original.

20. How are the angels involved in this discussion? Angels are God's messengers who minister to the saints (Daniel 9:21–23; 10:11–12). Since prophecy is a message from God, angels can be involved in this process. Angels also deliver answers to prayer (Daniel 6:22; Acts 12:7–11; Revelation 8:3–4). Angels apparently are constant observers of the believers' activities. Therefore, a woman with long hair has authority when she "prays or prophesies" (11:3). A woman who celebrates her femininity makes a statement to the Lord, the angels, and others in society. Women who cut their hair dishonor themselves (11:5). See more on "because of the angels" in David S. Norris's *Discovering God's Holiness* (2002).
21. Freeman, *Prophet*, 85.
22. Recommended resources on uncut hair include *My Hair, My Glory* by Juli Jasinski and *The Covering* by Lori Wagner.
23. Hayter, *The New Eve in Christ*, 125–26.
24. See use of *'ēzer* in Exodus 18:4; Deuteronomy 33:7, 26, 29; Psalm 20:2; 33:20; 70:5; Hosea 13:9; and many more. Also, John 14:26 conveys the same idea.

CHAPTER 11
HE CALLED RUTH: WOMEN AS WIVES

1. Ruth 4:13, 18–22; Matthew 1:5.
2. The Masoretic Text placed Ruth directly after Proverbs. See C. Marvin Pate, ed., *The Story of Israel: A Biblical Theology* (Downers Grove, Il: IVP Academic, 2004), 59.
3. A Ruth should fling herself on her Boaz. If a woman does not trust a man to provide for her and protect her, then she should not marry him. If a Boaz will not be brave enough to take a woman in front of God and fellow citizens and provide for her, he is not ready to marry.
4. Genesis 2:23–24; Ephesians 5:30–32. Much confusion about the role of women in the church comes from a lack of distinction between the home and the body of Christ. Just because a husband leads the home does not mean men must lead the church.
5. John H. Walton, *Genesis*, NIVAC (Grand Rapids, MI: Zondervan, 2001), 177.
6. James 4:1.
7. James 4:4.
8. Some have pointed out that some of these instructions to husbands/wives come in a few sets of "household codes" which also speak to slave/master relationships (See Schreiner, "Women," 304 referencing passages such as Ephesians 5:22–33 and 6:5–9; Colossians 3:18–19 and 3:22–4:1; Titus 2:4–5 and 2:9–10; I Peter 2:18–25 and 3:1–7.) They go on to argue that since slavery "no longer matters" then husband/wife statements are no longer binding either. The problem with that is the fact that within these lists also appear parent/child instructions. I certainly hope no one thinks children no longer need to obey their parents (although some teenagers would be glad to be told this). Furthermore, neither the instructions to the husband, master, or parent say to domineer, boss, or otherwise control others. Both those in leadership and those following are called to a humble servant spirit.
9. I Peter 3:6.
10. Name changed as I don't remember what it really was.
11. A man does not even have the right to divorce his wife. Jesus answered a question by hard-hearted religion experts who wanted to know if a man could issue a divorce. Jesus said that God made the male and female relationship. Man didn't invent marriage so he cannot deconstruct it either (Mark 10:2–9). Marriage is out of our control; it only works when we follow the One who invented it. We do not leave our spouses for the same reason Christ and the Church are inseparable. Our marriages preach this sermon.
12. Keener, *Acts*, 622–23.

13. Ibid., 621.
14. I Peter 3:7, emphasis added.
15. Eve misquoted God in Genesis 3:3. We only see the Lord instruct Adam about the tree in Genesis 2 before Eve was created. She did not know "God's Word."
16. Genesis 3:13 and II Corinthians 11:3 say that Eve was "beguiled" or tricked into what she did.
17. Karl-Wilhelm Westmeier, *Protestant Pentecostalism in Latin America* (Madison, NJ: Fairleigh Dickinson University, 1999), 107.
18. Mark McClintock, "Sis. Bernadine Caldwell—The ninetyandnine.com Interview," January 14, 2008, accessed November 16, 2011 http://www.ninetyandnine.com/Archives/20080114/cover.htm
19. The word for authority here is *exousiazō*. See I Corinthians 7:1–5 for context which speaks particularly about sexual relationships within marriage.
20. I Peter 5:3.
21. Schreiner, "Women," 288–307, in *Two Views*, ed. Beck.
22. Fred Kinzie, "The Story of Carl and Mable Hensley," *Profiles of Pentecostal Missionaries*, Mary Wallace, ed. (Hazelwood, MO: Word Aflame, 1986), 118–20, 134.
23. I Corinthians 7:28.
24. McClintock, "Bernadine Caldwell."
25. Ruth Senter, *Have We Really Come a Long Way?* (Minneapolis, MN: Bethany House, 1997), 19–20.
26. Ibid., 22.
27. Ruth first picked up leftover grain in the fields of Boaz. He gave her as much as she could gather of the harvest. When she became his wife, she was no longer on the edges, so to speak, but came into a central role.

CHAPTER 12

HE CALLED TABITHA: WOMEN AS ROLE-MODELS

1. "Dorcas," the Greek version of her name, also means 'gazelle.'
2. I Timothy 5:5.
3. Billy Cole, "Spiritual Warfare" (sermon, Alexandria, LA, 1990).
4. Romans 15:30; I Corinthians 1:11; Colossians 4:3; I Thessalonians 5:25; II Thessalonians 3:1–3.
5. This did not discourage her from home births, though. She's had the rest of them at home, too. And a midwife still has not been able to attend any of them!
6. Romans 14; I Corinthians 8; 10:16–33.

Bibliography

Anderson, Chris. "Eva Hunt: Pioneer of Home Missions." Unpublished paper for Urshan Graduate School of Theology. Accessed from carascall.com July 1, 2014. Apr 2003: 5.

Bailey, Kenneth E. *Paul Through Mediterranean Eyes: Cultural Studies in 1 Corinthians*. Downers Grove, IL: InterVarsity, 2011.

Bair, Barbara. "'Ethiopia Shall Stretch Forth Her Hands unto God': Laura Kofey and the Gendered Vision of Redemption in the Garvey Movement." *A Mighty Baptism: Race, Gender, and the Creation of American Protestantism*. Susan Juster and Lisa MacFarlane, ed. Ithaca, NY: Cornell, 1996.

Balsdon, J. P. V. D. *Roman Women: Their History and Habits*. London: Bodley Head, 1962.

Bauckham, Richard. *Gospel Women*. Grand Rapids, MI: Eerdmans, 2002.

Beck, James R., ed. *Two Views on Women in Ministry*. Revised. Grand Rapids, MI: Zondervan, 2005.

Bederman, Gail. "'The Women Have Had Charge of the Church Work Long Enough': The Men and Religion Forward Movement of 1911-1912 and the Masculinization of Middle-Class Protestantism." *A Mighty Baptism: Race, Gender, and the Creation of American Protestantism*. Susan Juster and Lisa MacFarlane, eds. Ithaca, NY: Cornell, 1996.

Belleville, Linda L. "Teaching and Usurping Authority." *Discovering Biblical Equality: Complementarity without Hierarchy*. Ronald W. Pierce and Rebecca Merrill Groothuis, eds. Downers Grove, IL: InterVarsity, 2004: 205–223.

_____. *Women Leaders and the Church*. Grand Rapids, MI: Baker, 2000.

Bernard, David K. *The Apostolic Life*. Hazelwood, MO: Word Aflame, 2006.

_____. *Spiritual Leadership in the Twenty-first Century: Advice for Ministers and Church Leaders*. Hazelwood, MO: Word Aflame, 2015.

Bilzekian, Gilbert. *Beyond Sex Roles*. Third edition. Grand Rapids, MI: Baker Academic, 2006.

Bridges, Linda McKinnish. "Women in Church Leadership." *Review and Expositor*. 95. Aug 1 1998: 325–347.

Bruce, F. F. *Commentary on the Book of Acts*. New International Commentary on the New Testament. Grand Rapids, MI: Eerdmans, 1977.

Bushnell, Katharine C. *God's Word to Women*. Minneapolis: Christians for Biblical Equality, 2003.

Clouse, Bonnidell and Robert C., eds. *Women in Ministry: Four Views*. Downers Grove, IL: InterVarsity, 1989.

Cole, Billy. "Spiritual Warfare." Sermon preached at Because of the Times, Alexandria, LA, 1990.

Doje, Kenter and Stanley Scism. *Little Lady*. Bridgton, MO: Wonderful Words, 1990.

Doriani, Dan. *Women and Ministry*. Wheaton, IL: Crossway, 2003.

Drost, Bill. *Bill Drost The Pentecost*. Hazelwood, MO: Word Aflame, 1983.

Ellingsworth, Doug. *Call Me Blessed*. Dyersburg, TN: Seven Orders, 2015.

Ellis, E. Earle. *Pauline Theology: Ministry and Society*. Grand Rapids, MI: Eerdmans, 1989.

Epp, Eldon J. *Junia: The First Woman Apostle*. Minneapolis, MN: Fortress, 2005.

Ewart, Frank J. *The Phenomenon of Pentecost*. Revised. Hazelwood, MO: Word Aflame, 2000.

Flanagan, Neal M. and Edwina H. Synder. "Did Paul Put Down Women in 1 Cor 14:34–36?" *Biblical Theology Bulletin*, 11, 1981: 10–12.

Freeman, Nona. *A Prophet in Our Time*. Minden, LA: Barnes, 2007.

_____. *Everything Is Gonna Be All Right*. Fort Worth, TX: n.p., 2005.

Goss, Ethel E. *The Winds of God*. Revised by Ruth Goss Nortjé. Hazelwood, MO: Word Aflame, 1977.

Grady, J. Lee. *10 Lies the Church Tells Women*. Lake Mary, FL: Charisma, 2006.

Grenz, Stanley J. *Women in the Church: A Biblical Theology of Women in Ministry*. Downers Grove, IL: InterVarsity, 1995.

Grudem, Wayne. *Evangelical Feminism & Biblical Truth: An Analysis of More than 100 Disputed Questions*. Revised. Wheaton, IL: Crossway, 2012.

_____. *Evangelical Feminism: a New Path to Liberalism?* Wheaton, IL: Crossway, 2006.

Hayter, Mary. *The New Eve in Christ: The Use and Abuse of the Bible in the Debate about Women in the Church*. Grand Rapids, MI: Eerdmans, 1987.

Hugenberger, Gordon P. "Women in Church Office: Hermeneutics or Exegesis? A Survey of Approaches to 1 Tim 2:8-15." *Journal of the Evangelical Theological Society*, 35/3, Sept 1992: 341–360.

Husbands, Mark and Timothy Larsen, eds. *Women, Ministry, and the Gospel: Exploring New Paradigms*. Downers Grove, IL: InterVarsity, 2007.

Huther, Johann Eduard. *Critical and Exegetical Hand-Book to the Epistles to Timothy and Titus*. Trans. from 4th edition of German by David Hunter. New York: Funk & Wagnalls, 1885.

Hyatt, Susan C. "Spirit-Filled Women." *Century of the Holy Spirit*. Vinson Synan, ed. Nashville: Thomas Nelson, 2001.

Jasinski, Juli. *Step Up—For Lady Preachers ONLY*. Hollis, NH: 2013.

Jeremias, Joachim. *Jerusalem in the Time of Jesus*. Philadelphia, PA: Fortress, 1969.

Jewett, Robert. "Paul, Phoebe, and the Spanish Mission." *The Social World of Formative Christianity and Judaism*. Jacob Neusner, et al., eds. Philadelphia, PA: Fortress, 1988.

Johnson, Luke T. *Reading Romans: A Literary and Theological Commentary*. New York: Crossroad, 1997.

Keener, Craig S. *1-2 Corinthians*. Cambridge, NY: Cambridge, 2005.

_____. *Acts: An Exegetical Commentary*. Vol. 1. Grand Rapids, MI: Baker, 2012.

_____. *Paul, Women and Wives*. Grand Rapids, MI: Zondervan, 1992.

Koren, Daniel. *Double Identity*. Neosho, MO: Living Springs, 2007.

_____. "Putting a Woman in Her Place: Females as Biblical Teachers, Elders, and Pastors." Master's thesis, Urshan Graduate School of Theology, 2014.

Kostenberger, Andreas J., and Thomas R. Schreiner. *Women in the Church: An Analysis and Application of 1 Timothy 2:9-15*. 2nd ed. Grand Rapids, MI: Baker, 2005.

Kroeger, Richard C. and Catherine C. *I Suffer Not a Woman: Rethinking 1 Timothy 2:11-15 in Light of Ancient Evidence*. Grand Rapids, MI: Baker, 1992.

Lindley, Susan Hill. *"You Have Stept Out of Your Place."* Louisville, KY: Westminster John Knox, 1996.

Metzger, Bruce M. *A Textual Commentary on the Greek New Testament*. Second edition. Fourth revised. New York: American Bible, 2002.

McClintock, Mark. "Sis. Bernadine Caldwell—The ninetyandnine.com Interview." Jan 14 2008 accessed Nov 16 2011 http://www.ninetyandnine.com/Archives/20080114/cover.htm

Morris, Joan. *The Lady Was a Bishop*. New York: Macmillan, 1973.

Norris, David S. *Discovering God's Holiness*. 2002.

_____. "Exploring the Glass Ceiling: Women Who Minister." Urshan Graduate School of Theology Symposium. Hazelwood, MO. 2003.

_____. "Finding Room in the Margins: A Historical Look at Pentecostal Women and Calling." Passing the Mantle Conference. Hazelwood, MO. 2007.

_____. "Prophesying Daughters." *Forward*. Fall 2009.

Odell-Scott, David W. "In Defense of an Egalitarian Interpretation of 1 Cor 14:34-36: A Reply to Murphy-O'Connor's Critique." *Biblical Theology Bulletin*. 17:3. 1987: 100–103.

_____. "Let the Women Speak in Church: An Egalitarian Interpretation of I Cor. 14:33b-36." *Biblical Theology Bulletin*. 13, 1983: 90–93.

Orr, J. Edwin. *The Fervent Prayer*. Chicago: Moody, 1974.

Pate, C. Marvin, ed. *The Story of Israel: A Biblical Theology*. Downers Grove, IL: IVP Academic, 2004.

Payne, Philip. "Libertarian Women in Ephesus: A Response to Douglas G. Moo's Article, 1 Timothy 2:11–15 Meaning and Significance." *Trinity Journal*. 2, 1981: 169–197.

Perriman, Andrew. *Speaking of Women*. Leicester, England: Apollos, 1998.

Pierce, Ronald W., and Rebecca Merrill Gruthuis, eds. *Discovering Biblical Equality*. Downers Grove, IL: InterVarsity, 2004.

Piper, John and Wayne Grudem, eds. *Recovering Biblical Manhood & Womanhood: A Response to Evangelical Feminism.* Wheaton, IL: Crossway, 1991.

Prohl, Russell C. *Woman in the Church: A Restudy of Woman's Place in Building the Kingdom.* Grand Rapids, MI: Eerdmans, 1957.

Quinn Jerome D., and William C. Wacker. *The First and Second Letters to Timothy.* Eerdmans Critical Commentary. Grand Rapids, MI: Eerdmans, 2000.

Randall, Ian. *Rhythms of Revival: The Spiritual Awakening of 1857–63.* Milton Keynes UK: Paternoster, 2010.

Shaw, Mark. *Global Awakening: How 20th-Century Revivals Triggered a Christian Revolution.* Downers Grove, IL: InterVarsity, 2010.

Smelser, Georgia. *Oma.* Hazelwood, MO: Word Aflame, 1981.

Spencer, Aida B. *Beyond the Curse: Women Called to Ministry.* Peabody, MA: Hendrickson, 1985.

Staton, Knofel. *The Biblical Liberation of Women for Leadership in the Church.* Eugene, OR: Wipf and Stock, 2003.

Sumner, Sarah. *Men and Women in the Church.* Downers Grove, IL: InterVarsity, 2003.

Swidler, Leonard. *Women in Judaism.* Metuchen, NJ: Scarecrow, 1976.

Synan, Vinson. *The Holiness-Pentecostal Movement in the United States.* Grand Rapids, MI: Eerdmans, 1971.

Tucker, Ruth A. *First Ladies of the Parish.* Grand Rapids, MI: Zondervan, 1988.

_____. *Women in the Maze: Questions & Answers on Biblical Equality.* Downers Grove, IL: InterVarsity, 1992.

Trombley, Charles. *Who Said Women Can't Teach?* South Plainfield, NJ: Bridge, 1985.

Tyson, James L. *The Early Pentecostal Revival.* Hazelwood, MO.: Word Aflame, 1992.

Walton, John H. *Genesis.* NIV Application Commentary. Grand Rapids, MI: Zondervan, 2001.

Wallace, Mary H., ed. *Pioneer Pentecostal Women.* Vol. 1. Hazelwood, MO: Word Aflame, 1981.

_____. *Pioneer Pentecostal Women.* Vol. 2. Hazelwood, MO: Word Aflame, 1981.

_____. *Profiles of Pentecostal Missionaries.* Hazelwood, MO: Word Aflame, 1986.

Westmeier, Karl-Wilhelm. *Protestant Pentecostalism in Latin America.* Madison, NJ: Fairleigh Dickinson University, 1999.

Wilshire, Leland E. *Insight into Two Biblical Passages.* Lanham, MD: University, 2010.

Witherington, Ben, III. *Conflict & Community in Corinth: A Socio-Rhetorical Commentary on 1 and 2 Corinthians.* Grand Rapids, MI: Eerdmans, 1995.

_____, and Darlene Hyatt. *Paul's Letter to the Romans: A Socio-Rhetorical Commentary.* Grand Rapids, MI: Eerdmans, 2004.

_____. *Women and the Genesis of Christianity.* New York: Cambridge, 1990.

Womble, T. Scott. *Beyond Reasonable Doubt: 95 Theses which Dispute the Church's Conviction Against Women.* Xulon, 2008.

Wynn, Prathia Hall. "Foreword." *Those Preachin' Women: Sermons by Black Women Preachers.* Ella Pearson Mitchell, ed. Valley Forge, VA: Judson, 1985.

Zens, Jon. *What's with Paul and Women? Unlocking the Cultural Background to 1 Timothy 2.* Lincoln, NE: Ekklesia, 2010.

Scripture Index

Genesis 1:27	134	I Samuel 9:6–10	184
Genesis 1:27–28	196	Esther 7:2	89
Genesis 1:28	85, 131	Psalm 20:2	197
Genesis 2	198	Psalm 33:20	197
Genesis 2:21–23	131	Psalm 70:5	197
Genesis 2:23–24	197	Proverbs 31	xiii
Genesis 3:3	198	Proverbs 31:10	148
Genesis 3:6	85, 132	Proverbs 31:10–12	147
Genesis 3:13	198	Daniel 6:22	197
Genesis 3:16	159	Daniel 9:21–23	197
Genesis 4:7	159	Daniel 10:11–12	197
Genesis 21:12	189	Hosea 13:9	197
Exodus 3:12	179	Joel 2:28	34
Exodus 15:20–21	182	Joel 2:28–29	29
Exodus 18:4	197	Matthew 1:5	197
Exodus 19:6	179	Matthew 5:28	21
Exodus 38:8	182	Matthew 6:26	189
Deuteronomy 5:5	179	Matthew 7:15–20	194
Deuteronomy 24:1–4	194	Matthew 8:8–9	191
Deuteronomy 33:7	197	Matthew 13:31–33	182
Judges 4:4–5	47	Matthew 15:2	183
Judges 4:17–22	185	Matthew 16:19	191
Judges 5:24–27	185	Matthew 18:18–20	191
Ruth 3:11	148	Matthew 19:11–12	194
Ruth 4:13	197	Matthew 19:28	181
I Samuel 2:22	182	Matthew 20:6–7	x

Matthew 20:20	182	Luke 13:14	195
Matthew 20:25–28	91	Luke 13:20	181
Matthew 21:23	191	Luke 15:8	181
Matthew 21:23–27	183	Luke 16:18	188
Matthew 21:31–32	21	Luke 17:35	181
Matthew 21:32	21	Luke 20:8	183
Matthew 23:2–6	183	Luke 22:30	181
Matthew 23:6–12	196	Luke 24:1–11	21
Matthew 24:37–41	182	Luke 24:6–7	22
Matthew 28:1–10	21	Luke 24:9–12	182
Matthew 28:1–8	182	Luke 24:10	180
Matthew 28:5–7	186	Luke 24:11	182
Matthew 28:10	22	John 1:1–2	134
Matthew 28:19	193	John 4	26
Mark 4:28	190	John 4:19–26	186
Mark 6:23	92	John 4:36	193
Mark 7:3	183	John 4:39	25
Mark 7:5–13	183	John 10:5	x
Mark 10:2–9	197	John 13:5	196
Mark 10:5–9	194	John 14:26	197
Mark 10:12	194	John 20:1–18	182
Mark 10:45	192	John 20:10–18	21
Mark 15:41	21, 182	John 21:15–17	195
Mark 16:1–11	182	Acts 1:11	187
Luke 1:19	183	Acts 2	30
Luke 1:34	188	Acts 6:1–5	193
Luke 1:41–55	183	Acts 6:1–7	192
Luke 1:46–56	22	Acts 7:60	183
Luke 2:36	188	Acts 8:1–3	183
Luke 2:36–37	182	Acts 8:5–13	193
Luke 2:36–38	29	Acts 8:19	191
Luke 4:6	191	Acts 9:2	183
Luke 4:18	182	Acts 9:14	191
Luke 4:23–27	182	Acts 9:26	191
Luke 7:8	191	Acts 9:36–41	169
Luke 7:36–50	21	Acts 12:7–11	197
Luke 8:1–3	21, 182	Acts 12:12	187, 192, 195
Luke 8:3	5, 20	Acts 13:1	187, 194
Luke 9:22	22	Acts 13:15	195
Luke 10:1	180	Acts 15:38–39	194
Luke 10:34–35	192	Acts 16:13	139
Luke 10:38–42	17	Acts 16:13–15	115
Luke 10:39	21		

Scripture Index | 207

Acts 16:14–15	192	Romans 16:13	195
Acts 16:40	187	I Corinthians 1:11	198
Acts 17:24	189	I Corinthians 1:26	182
Acts 18	183, 187	I Corinthians 3:5	192–3
Acts 18:2	185	I Corinthians 3:5–8	193
Acts 18:18	185	I Corinthians 3:9	187
Acts 18:25–26	187	I Corinthians 4:17	187
Acts 18:26	185	I Corinthians 5	191
Acts 19:21–41	190	I Corinthians 6:12	40
Acts 19:23–41	190	I Corinthians 6:12–13	183
Acts 19:34	190	I Corinthians 7:1–5	198
Acts 20:17	194	I Corinthians 7:10	188
Acts 20:28	194	I Corinthians 7:26	187
Acts 20:29–30	190	I Corinthians 7:28	198
Acts 20:30	195	I Corinthians 7:4	162
Acts 21:33–35	186	I Corinthians 8	198
Acts 21:8	183	I Corinthians 9:10	183
Acts 22:2	186	I Corinthians 9:6	180
Acts 26:10	191	I Corinthians 11	132–33, 136, 139, 141
Acts 28:23	187		
Romans 1:13	179		
Romans 2:18	187	I Corinthians 11:3	197
Romans 5:12–19	190	I Corinthians 11:5	197
Romans 7:6	183	I Corinthians 11:10	137
Romans 8:29	179	I Corinthians 11:15	142, 196
Romans 12:8	192, 194	I Corinthians 11:2	36
Romans 14	198	I Corinthians 11:3	183
Romans 14:4	23	I Corinthians 11:4–7	140
Romans 15:30	198	I Corinthians 11:6	184
Romans 15:8	192	I Corinthians 11:7	142
Romans 15:9	193	I Corinthians 11:8	136
Romans 16	5, 71, 104, 192, 105, 192	I Corinthians 12	38
		I Corinthians 12:8–10	183, 187
Romans 16:1		I Corinthians 12:28	6, 33, 70
Romans 16:1–12	71		
Romans 16:1–2	103, 192	I Corinthians 13:4–8	185
Romans 16:3	180, 185, 187	I Corinthians 14	37, 39
		I Corinthians 14:6	187
Romans 16:3–4	59, 187	I Corinthians 14:21	183
Romans 16:6	187	I Corinthians 14:34–36	183
Romans 16:7	1, 5, 187	I Corinthians 14:13	60
		I Corinthians 14:19	187

Reference	Pages
I Corinthians 14:24–25	60
I Corinthians 14:34	30, 65
I Corinthians 14:34–35	vii, 29, 31, 33–35, 37, 39, 51, 62, 183, 185–186
I Corinthians 14:6	38
I Corinthians 14:37	185
I Corinthians 15:7	180
I Corinthians 15:32	190
I Corinthians 15:46	190
I Corinthians 16:15	187
I Corinthians 16:16	154, 188
I Corinthians 16:19	185
II Corinthians 1:24	187, 191
II Corinthians 3:6	193
II Corinthians 6:1–13	192
II Corinthians 6:4	193
II Corinthians 8:23	180, 187
II Corinthians 11:13–15	190
II Corinthians 11:23	193
II Corinthians 11:3	190, 198
Galatians 2:16	183
Galatians 3:25	183
Galatians 3:28	137
Galatians 5:1	183
Galatians 6:6	187
Ephesians 3:1	192
Ephesians 3:7	193
Ephesians 4:1	192
Ephesians 4:11	6, 187, 194
Ephesians 4:11–16	137
Ephesians 4:12	109, 119
Ephesians 4:15–16	136
Ephesians 5:11–12	184
Ephesians 5:22	81, 154
Ephesians 5:22–33	189, 197
Ephesians 5:25–33	151
Ephesians 5:30–32	197
Ephesians 6:5–9	197
Ephesians 6:12	191
Ephesians 6:21	193
Ephesians 6:21–22	192
Philippians 2:14	188
Philippians 2:25	180, 187
Philippians 2:25–30	192
Philippians 2:3–7	152
Philippians 3:2–3	194
Philippians 4:2–3	180
Philippians 4:3	71, 180
Colossians 1:7	193
Colossians 1:15	134
Colossians 2:19	136
Colossians 3:16	68, 187
Colossians 3:18–19	197
Colossians 3:22–4:1	197
Colossians 4:7	193
Colossians 4:11	180
Colossians 4:15	187, 192
Colossians 4:3	198
Colossians 4:7–9	192
I Thessalonians 1:1	187
I Thessalonians 2:7	101
I Thessalonians 3:2	180, 187
I Thessalonians 4:16–17	190
I Thessalonians 5:12	192
I Thessalonians 5:12–13	192
I Thessalonians 5:25	198
II Thessalonians 3:1–3	198
II Thessalonians 3:11–12	186
I Timothy	65, 79
I Timothy 1:3	63, 186
I Timothy 1:4	190
I Timothy 1:19–20	190
I Timothy 1:20	195
I Timothy 2	75, 79, 81
I Timothy 2:2	65, 186
I Timothy 2:8	79
I Timothy 2:8–15	80
I Timothy 2:9–10	80
I Timothy 2:9–15	189

Reference	Pages
I Timothy 2:11	81, 190
I Timothy 2:11–12	vii, 63, 64, 67, 72, 75, 87, 140, 186, 188, 189, 193
I Timothy 2:11–15	86
I Timothy 2:12	87, 90, 186, 189, 195
I Timothy 2:13	83
I Timothy 3	121, 123, 193
I Timothy 3:1	120, 194
I Timothy 3:2	120–122, 187, 195
I Timothy 3:4	122
I Timothy 3:4–5	192, 194
I Timothy 3:8–13	106
I Timothy 3:9–12	195
I Timothy 3:10	190
I Timothy 4:1	190
I Timothy 4:3	75
I Timothy 4:7	125
I Timothy 4:12	128
I Timothy 4:13	187
I Timothy 4:14	57, 195
I Timothy 5:1–2	127, 195–6
I Timothy 5:5	124, 187, 198
I Timothy 5:17	192
I Timothy 5:18	195
I Timothy 5:19–20	195
I Timothy 5:9	193
I Timothy 5:15	190
I Timothy 5:18	195
I Timothy 6:20	190
II Timothy 2:1–2	186
II Timothy 2:2	186–7
II Timothy 2:16	187, 190
II Timothy 3:5	187
II Timothy 3:6	195
II Timothy 4:4	190
II Timothy 4:19	185
II Timothy 4:2	195
Titus 1	123
Titus 1:5	195
Titus 1:5–7	125
Titus 1:10–11	187
Titus 2:2	186
Titus 2:2–5	125
Titus 2:3	63, 110, 126, 187
Titus 2:3–5	170, 193
Titus 2:4	126, 176, 190
Titus 2:4–5	193, 195, 197
Titus 2:7	128
Titus 2:9–10	197
Titus 2:23	195
Titus 3:8	192
Titus 3:9	190
Titus 3:10–11	187
Philemon 1–2	187
Philemon 24	180
Philemon 9	101
Philemon 24	187
Hebrews 1:3	196
Hebrews 5:6	179
Hebrews 5:12	70
Hebrews 6:20	179
Hebrews 7:11	179
Hebrews 11:11	87
Hebrews 12:15	120
Hebrews 13:7	191
Hebrews 13:17	98
James 2:5	182
James 3:17	190
James 4:1	197
James 4:4	197
James 5:14	195
I Peter 2:18–25	197
I Peter 2:21	196

I Peter 3	75, 81
I Peter 3:1–2	80
I Peter 3:1–6	73, 79, 80
I Peter 3:1–7	197
I Peter 3:3–6	76
I Peter 3:6	197
I Peter 3:7	198
I Peter 4:10–11	178
I Peter 5:2	194–195
I Peter 5:2–4	124
I Peter 5:3	198
I Peter 5:5	154
I John 2:13–14	193, 195
II John 1	126
III John 4	126
Revelation 2:14	191
Revelation 2:20–23	191
Revelation 8:3–4	197
Revelation 12:12–14	181